C0-AQI-364

Vault

—

Alice Jones

Apogee Press

Berkeley · California

2020

Acknowledgements

Thanks to Patricia Dienstfrey, Rusty Morrison and Francis Martineau
for their comments on the manuscript. And thanks to the editors and staffs
of the following journals where earlier versions of the poems appeared.

Boston Review – Idyll, Vault, Evolution
Colorado Review – O
Denver Quarterly – Membrane
Hotel Amerika – Vision
Interim – Fire, Milk and Honey
Narrative Magazine – Oracle, Spell
New American Writing – Crystal Objects
Parthenon West – E, I, Sometimes Y
Verse – Blackbird, Calligraphy, Hole, Limit, A, Pith, Vines
Volt – Darkling I listen, Tongue
"Spell" won the First Annual Poetry Prize from *Narrative Magazine*.

©2020 by Alice Jones

ISBN 978-1-7331375-1-5. Library of Congress Control Number: 2019955349.

Book design by Philip Krayna, Conifer Creative
www.conifercreative.com

Published by Apogee Press
2308 Sixth Street
Berkeley, CA 94710
www.apogeepress.com

Table of Contents

A

Unfathomable mind, now beacon, now sea.
—Samuel Beckett

Door, door opening on every pulse, the same empty hall,
washed and unlit, the same peculiar night lit by green planets,

cradled on the inspired breath, one O, another,
the circle we emerged from, blood and muscle, space

without sphincter, she pushed, we came. Hello? Sound tunnels
from one world to the next, sometimes the line goes dead.

The unthought scheme of things, design, circle to circle,
continent's end—the skin shelf of nothing beyond what's seeable

from here, Circe's song, the sirens' wail, the ear's small cave,
lips' vermillion rim, apart, the world comes, I came, she. Then

hunger's clawed hand, the reach towards an iron door,
penitentiary, century of penitence, patience of the buried

furless creature. Iron innocence, barely light, your breath pulsing
little tides, mornings left, how many? day shaking itself awake.

The long-lined infinitesimal pin-pricked light, the stars are holes.
Black sled, so fast, s-curves, the silk, the sail, satin undies,

"smalls" they're called. Who wanted you? For the long feathers,
pinions, bead-heads, the father's reach, how far the wrenching,

unheard secrets, questions a child's mind forms around:
kernel of nothing that becomes the something inside

of each who, where. A voice opens like water, the pour
overboard, the poor filling the world, the world refusing

to fill them. Landscape develops rilles, loamy with tendrils,
the scent of wet earth seeping, that's where we'll go soon,

manacled to time—you're it, the body pulls you along. Spill
out a line into a place that isn't there yet, are you singing?

Won't, far-fetched, water pail, mooncalf, milk in the face,
a wake is full of food, the dead aren't talking, can't, they lie there

listening to us chew, those pink spotted star lilies that smell
too strong. Possibility always open, we turn from it so often,

a window, and then one orange day gone into the rumpled
flannel of a Sunday and where are you? The spotted hand,

lost ring, sweet unlived days, pool of mind, welcome water,
drink, lap, the slip-flap turnings of desire, wake up, padding,

row row under the wavelets under the covers, slip slip, in we go.
The Cha'am salmon? Something spicy, cilantro, walk in

the kite-flying marina, purple darkness oozing in, open skin,
a mind's easing itself up and over the lip of time. Small daily

killing, desire unfolding all over again inside the slipknot's loop,
stepping down the mossy stairs into the bottle-green bay, who is it?

No one. Me? Black is a quality of space, vibrations lengthen
into flood, the wash, the sea. Who went there? The ones who came

before, the embryo, the vanished, gone, the sunk and sinking.
What peace is there at this point? Peach-lit fog blows in, scrawling,

we go over the edge again, who said ground is basic? "Myriad-minded,"
shapely, ship-shape, formless, figure and arc, the reach into—

what do you figure? Drift grasses, black oolong, sip air and otherness, one
conceivable line of time. It floored me, what was there, disguised as nothing:

a wall of water, silver surface, creased and wind-driven, sun-stricken,
almost painful, from the massive heavenly dark, down here, shining.

Blackbird

You wanted a life formed like something recognizable, not amoeboid, not a platypus
(Europeans who first saw one took it for a hoax). Expecting shape, you got dream and

waking intermingled, a world of murder, one retro-fitted house, two weak ankles, starving
children looking out at you from each day's world news, a ridiculous series of cohabiting cats,

undefinable work, the Pacific nearby, blue globe going belly up, killing ourselves with all
we own, self-love, field-workers picking our breakfast fruits, blackberry canes taking over

the garden, Miles playing "So what?" One live love, one frayed, one dead: improbability
becomes you. Do without simplicity, do without everything, even bone. My workday's

unfolding, reaching into word work/word play, terrible fixes, as if trying to enact what can't
be named, high flung drama, sorry predicaments, our small daily insanities. It's not so much

setting a mind right as trying to name what's wrong, being known, accompanying
in language. Small chattering black birds sitting on the high wire, resting there, perched

without effort, let themselves fall off, glide, catch the arc at its lowest point, then loft.
Going with what is. The platypus hatches her eggs in a burrow, babies emerge the size

of lima beans, lap up nippleless mother's milk from abdominal folds, find food by
generating electric fields, ancient, Gondwana-borne. No one planned this.

Conversation with my father: How could you vote for someone who does not believe
in evolution? Really? He'll now tell his friends. Walking in the pine woods,

at nine or ten, finding a perfectly preserved mouse skull half-buried in the needles,
vacated cranial vault, come and gone, a life, one buzzing soul we all inhabit

while pretending to be separate selves. The non-human has its consciousness
too. Last week they found a coastal shrub that recognizes members of its own species,

grows differently in contact, as if mindful of community. Nested here among the piles
of books, loose paper, scraps, the cat who wants to lie on top of whatever I'm looking at,

gaze-warmed, rests his half-orange head on a corner of *Portrait of the Artist*. Coming back
from the beach, my sun-blistered nose would shape up into a large green bleb, under-

tow, wave-tossed and abraded, digging sand out of scalp with fingers, crab, bottom-
dweller, garbage-eater, shit-dipper, seaweed oozing and dangling won't let go, life is easy

when you're not disturbed about the line between the living and the dead. The snow falls
everywhere, a ghost in the mother's heart becomes her child's heart, and the boy wonders

what is the empty pit at the center that makes everything mean nothing. Or, now a man,
he feels no pulse, no movement in his daughter's eyes; people who walk around appearing

to be alive, even capable. Geraniums come in all colors and sizes, I like the little burgundy one,
chocolaty, almost black which runs and spreads, variable and improbable, life forms and death

forms, intermingling like water, like stew (*boeuf en daube*). At work, up against the edges
of non-being, wondering how some people manage to hold themselves in the world when

everything is pushing elsewhere, away. Growing more still, barely breathing, she said she was
at the bottom of a black lake. The she who is no one and no one ever saw opens her mouth

to breath in mud. At the bottom of the well, no stars, nothing but frog-chirp, body-bellows
calling for a mate, no answer, maybe some ear hears, a small tympanic drum vibrates

in response to throat vibration and we call that song, lyrical-spherical, going under,
freshwater well, once a common Chinese form of suicide. Delusions. He asked what

did it mean that the stamp for his postcard was a picture of a blackbird like the one caught
in the chimney, why did I always wear a black dress, why did I not remove the grain

of rice lodged in his throat for two years. He told about hiding in the jungle when
noisy villagers came to burn down the family house, he still heard their voices, days

without food, kite-fighting in Rangoon, rubbing crushed glass on the string to cut
the others' cords. He left me a message on his way to the bridge—"Today is the day I die."

Vines

Vines, tendrils, lotus-like orange blooms with purple centers, splayed into blue,
the bay, vernal air, Mount Tamalpais, expanse stretched over afternoon, we focus

inward, press and curl. It almost doesn't matter that the flesh hangs in new ways
off the bone, architecture becomes character or the other way around. I meant that

I would be flesh with you as long as we're bodies, knowing time's numbers. Unraveled,
bone reflected in the silver Mexican mirror, levolor-lifted refractions, sailboat race

out on the bay means white, yellow, blue triangles set against darker blue, wind riffled
and glazed, blue-flanneled bed means love is the thing with lips, utter at outer moments.

We came here. Stretch and you'll fall off the bed, rumpled down, winter melon,
morning becomes us. Dream broke into rhythm, sound into image, mother into

longing, lover into all you inspired and over that... The mad cat's white fur is larger
than his body, spare room, where a mother would hold him by the scruff of the neck.

Walking on the slippery wet eucalyptus leaves, we slid down a canyon after the trail
vanished, overland, Tilden large enough to get lost in. Inside. Between. Chinese has

no prepositions, so our position is imaginary, black ink on white scroll, stitched
brocade background, the elder's words about nothing, "what seems like something

isn't." If I put these lines inside of those, sense occurs; if I put my skin alongside of
yours, sense undoes. Minutes, composed of the interchange of sameness and difference:

the fit of us without language, the long bones jut, fingers furl and uncurl, my ulnas,
your femurs, what's where, skin pulls with extra room made for pulling and careening

around as if we were other than imagined. Green vase, dried trumpet grass, so bell-like
it can't be real. Undone by trafficking in senses. Cradle and curry, the wide round-abouts

in Delhi, camel and elephant, old vines, passionflower, we ate chapati and raita, chicken
tikka masala, made the chutney myself, now they say turmeric prevents dementia. Jade,

smooth as enamel, hangs warmly between breasts, green moon, poor toes, moorings
lost, that's why we came here, incense ash, rose oil, we elapse, hand eclipses eye, today's

ellipsis. Tess sleeping her last night at Stonehenge, a heathen in her own skin at last. Who
named you? The calligrapher's grandfather. Spring rain means yellow, means king of

the large belly, brings East and West into one cipher, wild tangle, the circle, yin-yang—
now a western cliché. Rain doesn't come here, crows do, temples show some undarkening,

brown spots on the backs of hands, can those be removed? Time put them. Maybe cure
with cream, the erasing one. Heat generated under thick quilt, cold ankles and fingers.

Wildcat Peak at orange sun-down, pink under-scudded clouds against lavender, painted
like a nursery. Strong legs and their distance, we came here purposefully, walking uphill.

Calligraphy

Grass, slippery and spear-shaped, careful, don't crush, who said keep off the vast, soft
ecologically unsound terrain, blades, well-armed in number, seed-free replicants,

a clone's mammoth uncouth amplitude, go forth and multiply. Increase and desist,
the old men at the table remembering their youth in Hong Kong. At school they'd pen

the classics, hours of brush on ink-stone, a man's character said to be visible in his strokes,
a man's attainment seen in black wash on rice paper. One in a wheelchair, 91, the other

has lost all his present mind but amiably holds the old. Children gone gray, we are they,
looking at photos of the parents in cheongsams and chic sunglasses, 1952, Hong Kong.

The dapper young artillery colonel has gone deaf, he won't speak to his eldest daughter,
the angry son won't speak to us, jealousies abound and roil over years. I married the one

the grandfather adored, the father berated, the mother forgot. Walking on the edge
of the continent, we tour with cousins, palms and cacti point like bloated dinosaurs

in the Huntington Library gardens, strange fusion of botany and book museum. Facing
the door is a Gutenberg bible on vellum; a hand-copied prologue to the *Wife of Bath's*

Tale; first folio, "Stand and unfold yourself"; Armillary Sphere, Santucci, 1580, with Earth,
Moon, Mercury, Venus, Sun, Uranus, Jupiter, Saturn as the order was then perceived;

Hooke's *Micrographia*, an engraving of a transparent flea enlarged a thousand times;
Darwin's notebook, letters from Whitman, Lincoln, Dickinson. Text evolved on its medium

of vellum, dried and pounded skin, or paper, moist fibers of wood (xylem, phloem), grass,
rag, pressed into sheets. First writing: cuneifom, six millenia ago, Mesopotamian; Chinese

oracle bones, 6000 BCE; hieroglyphics, 3200 BCE; Indus script; first alphabets, Egyptian, Semitic, Phoenician, the Greeks added vowels; brush, stylus, quill, pencil, pen; functional

illiteracy, now 23%. Driving south towards the uncles, I listen to my mother on the phone, her voice creaks with fear, the neurologist said the little stroke she'd thought her husband

had was not a stroke—grade 4 glioblastoma. "In one month expect him to be in a wheelchair, in two months—gone." Hard for her to believe the man sitting calmly doing his crossword

in ink is so tenuously here. On the third anniversary, at the cemetery on a green hill in Whittier, each bows in turn to the aunt's granite plaque in the ground, flowers, in the old

land we'd have incense and torn paper remembrances to disperse in ash. Soil or fire or ocean, I can't decide anymore. A body careens dumbly, eloquently, freely, going heavenward into

jeremiad, keening, lamenting melancholy; nothing observes perfect quietude, restful silence; thought uses vastness, wanting Xanadu's youthful zeal. At Dai Gu Ma's graveside, waiting

for his time to lie down beside her, Uncle Di Gu Jeung, his Buddha-face unlined, sits and recalls her thrift, managing loans for her children's schools, her stories, fleeing warlords, she walked

with mother and brother and sister into the mainland seeing beheaded bodies by the roadside. Fleeing the Japanese, dressed as a man to not be raped, later fleeing the Communists who had

tortured their uncle, pretending to take him out in front of the firing squad each morning, making him kneel on broken glass to confess, the family mind inscribed with generations

of pain. At the museum, a poem in grass-script by Tang era Li Po (Cantonese Lei Bah, white plum). In the early dynasties, Jiǎvǎgǔwén characters were carved on bone, later silk

or bamboo; Cai Lun, Han Dynasty eunuch involved in palace intrigue, watched wasps
and bees build and so took rags and plant fiber to make paper. Surface on which to scratch,

Leonardo's left-handed writing in mirror-image cursive, notebooks of lists, plans,
whirlpools, dissections of fetus in utero, an opened heart, cross-sectioned skull, drawings

of the proportional man, the rhombicuboctahedron. Biji, Tang dynasty anecdote notebooks;
in Japan, Kenko's *Essays in Idleness*, zuihitsu, essays on random topics which "follow the impulse

of the brush." (Kimiko Hahn) Tenth century Japan, calligraphers began to paste text on paper
onto larger surfaces, though collage, from French, *coller*, to glue, had been around since

the Chinese invention of paper, used for tomb-rubbings, ink-washed. The absent ancestors
held close at hand by landowners, texture for holding memory, ghost-uncles, in constant

exile, moving on, "nor all thy piety nor wit / shall lure it back to cancel half a line / nor all
thy tears wash out a word of it." (Omar Khayyam) A boy's calligraphic designs, endlessly,

fluidly graphed, high-handed ink, jotted knots, liquid markings, notations of penmanship,
quixotic relaxed sentences, tangled usages, variations wander, xylem, yarrow, zigzag.

Membrane

Low gold on pine trunks, coastal grasses, the branched path of today's walk, last week's, last year's, time-layered and forked, the circle deepens, returned again, forgetting where

we went, except the master map on the basement wall remembers, black-lined charting, spider-web lines, our trails in the headlands, Pt. Reyes, water district, East Bay, golden-furred

felt-skinned summer hills, waiting for green December, we're thirsty. Drinking in, no one knew how far down the liquid went, intestinal gully, what fortress found a wall wanting.

Where is the inside? Who is it from? The cradle, crypt, the cock-a-doodle-do of morning's want-to-be song. Get up, say something, articulate a position that will orient the poor reader

to the ground, drain of the washed and wanted, the longed for and forgotten. Huge regret over who was left behind when they could have been brought along with us into the next circle,

a cookie in the pocket for when everyone starts to get a little tired. Chartreuse Nalgene hooked to the day pack, do we need to worry about polycarbonates? They found them in breast milk,

no line to divide what's eaten from what's supposed to stay outside, like weather, dust, dirt, decay. Dropped out from college and temporarily living in the Oregon woods, I received

a note from my mother with only one line—Remember about germs. Cellular envelope, molecular layers, fluid mosaic membrane, as if each lamina is a honeycomb through which

chemicals make their way, freeze-fracture electron microscopy looks like lunar geography, the inert taken in by pinocytosis, to be recognized as foreign by the white cell, surrounded,

ingested, merged with lysozymes, internal poisons used to digest outside poisons so I'm still me with as little dilution from the world as possible: delusion. The ultimate goal of the cell is to reproduce itself. Everything permeates everywhere, no safe enclave, not what I was told growing up in a homogenous zone. At the bat mitzvah of my Chinese husband's daughter,

her mother told the story of Jessie at six explaining to her Hebrew class how baby Moses was found floating down the Yangtze River, perfect sense, myths, gene pool, molecules mixing,

evolutionary leaps. Rocking basket, woven of river reeds carried by a current to pharaoh's daughter, found among the grasses, one way to explain the arrival of an unexpected baby.

Who carried him? Is a mother the one who breast feeds, the amah who wakes in the night, the one whose language you learn before the language of your parents? Cross-pollination makes

for hardiness, or, the hard-hearted world rejects hybrids? "I have upheld the hypothesis that the ego is constituted as a containing envelope, a protective barrier and a filter of exchanges,

as a result of proprioceptive and epidermal sensations and the internalization of skin identifications." (D. Anzieu, *The Skin Ego*) Dream: going forward on a tricycle whose front

wheel is turned backwards, trying not to drop the cross-eyed baby with his misshapen head. Directionality is over-rated, so try to do without for awhile, you'll see what I mean.

Happenstance and wherewithal, withdrawal is a lousy method, so we keep what we can in the bank. She said she has four embryos in storage, everyone is over-drawn or living

on equity or credit cards, money that isn't, walking on air, falling down stairs. The pocket is an interesting invention. The marsupials' two vaginas and two-pronged penises, which

do not pee given the cloaca for eliminating waste, tiny babies crawl up the mother's body to find the nipple in a pouch and cling for weeks. The girl put her hand into his pocket and

touched his cold fingers coming to life in the memory of Joyce's young Dedalus. The un-dead
are us, hold and hide, bottom lint, loose coins, bus transfer, used kleenex, lipstick,

at the party, I park my things inside his pocket since my dress has none, womb from
which comes forth garbage and objects which have outlived their everyday usage.

Mucilage will help us stick together, we're used to scattering. Fly and coalesce, sail off
and congregate, disperse and return to the house of one being, the everything we can't

imagine but trail around in. They discovered a batch of planets, 45 near suns, found
without the wobble-technique, locating now some smaller more imaginably habitable

places somebody might like to call home. Will your grandchildren live there? Add
water, microbes, create an ecosphere, chemicals that need each other and interdigitate,

branched proteins, permeable membranes, you have to learn to be separate in order to be
together. It took time to figure out that merger doesn't solve solitude. Side by side on a Big Sur

hillside the day before lightning started the big fire in the canyon's unwatered brush, our
shoulders almost touching but not quite, we watch the sun's mass puddle on a blue horizon.

E

Breath sealed inside a breath, held in salt, on a rubber cord,
the echo inside yourself of those who died before, whose place

you took inside the four directions, the 28 lunar mansions,
the dipper mother, sailing out underneath the orange gate,

flood tide, buoy bell marker. The ghost in parquetted halls,
barbed fences, flung window, persimmon tree, an ocean

where you found a voice speaking, a protea flowering for
the first time, solstice wobbling in. We sew and unsew,

dangled thread, the dish ran away, happenstance
and not, the docked loons, waving reeds, for many moons

we waited for the arrival of the silvered creature whose word
would open the unopened. A Taoist belief—writing is based

on unstable energy existing before matter—talismanic—
The Shrine of Numinous Response (repose). We floated,

fool, trouble fuels memory, not empty / not full, the in-between
place, lost, unfounded, assumptions of grandeur, enjoy

the delusions. Elevation desired and sinking, the crash
saves you. You flew away into yourself, ruffled feathers,

getting under someone's skin. "Since they take no credit
success remains with them." Procession of immortals

(mistakes, minerals) pay homage to the primordial. Always,
there isn't any. On the wing, flying off into everyday madness,

mired, mirrored, long spoons, purple trees leaving, the black cat
lost, goodbye, only one sphere, edges melding, peripheral

and silly. "The value in water benefits all things and yet
it does not contend." Reach for dark orange, the rose in full leaf,

green beach grasses, dawn, the zeeing bats, urgent sun won't sit
and wait like an egg: a beak pecks through, fractures, and then

the struggle of wet feathers begins in earnest. Breathing aims
so much life, molecular pulse, aspiration, aeration, the sleeves

rolled up and the nape soaked in its own sweat. Change—
the moon goddess lives in a great cold palace, trigrams,

dragons, chanting such as "Abnormal—in the shape of pigs,
cats, dogs or all those who eat their own young... " The value

in a mind, a square jar, only island. Bird gyre—swoop and beak—
the fine-feathered exit, swallow-tail blue, smooth and riparian.

Vision

He likes his Leica much more than the Nikon, icon of sharp focus, lenses ground clean.
Sight, hard-edged as glass. Swimming backstroke in the wind, droplets rain down like

flecks of bright mica, light of the air enters aquatic light, sinks into oneness. The mind
links everything it likes, while the "I" superimposes opinions. Surprising, how one can

distinguish type-faces having only a few microns of difference. In picong, said to be
like calypso, verbal taunts can't quite cross the line into insult; words that should be play

are wounding, dance of thrust and retreat, knife-edged verbiage, a likeness to syncopation
in which like-minded speakers collaborate and battle. Lilac, which is rare around here,

blooms for us each anniversary. Limax, the great gray or leopard slug is known for its unusual
mating: the pair circle and lick for hours unlike species who perform the act in a picosecond,

they dangle themselves from high trees by a mucous thread, entwine penis-like organs which
emerge from one side of the head and exchange sperm. Sometimes one eats the penis of

the other but they can continue to mate using female parts. Too much limelight is a bad thing,
visual relief, standing out from the many in high contrast, as Dickinson said, "It has a sting."

Swing from fine threads in the warm Caribbean breezes, bring your camera, we'll lick salt
from our wounds, silly fish, chimera, spread like mycelia, everywhere on earth, into each crack

and pore, each particular realm of being and undoing. Soil, so much worm-shit and water,
particulate and refractive in mineral content. Lumex, little new wide-angle digital camera

holds a Leica lens. One item missing from *Leaves of Grass* was the ligule, delicate hair found
at the junction of leaf blade and sheath, it encircles and claps the stem, erotic grasp. This site

distinguishes species, point of emergence. I was you, I liked being one thing, then we get up
wrapped in invisible threads, being separate beings, folded over on ourselves like pirozhki,

variations of gyoza or mandoo or karanji, ravioli, lumpia, jiaozi, my little dumpling. You must
be eating your burnt toast again, the smell wakes me at 3, I can never sleep through it, spoils

to the insomniacs, compost to the rest. The library lion wears a too-proud look, as if his pedestal
were a pile of encyclopedias, while inside dust mites vanish inside the frothy lungs of readers,

so different from the Hong Kong lions we photographed, small with knobby heads, protruding
dragon-eyes, fierce incisors, round clawed paws, one on each side of a gold-colored gate. We're

blind to all we hoped for, all we gave up on, fluorescent or unlit, no incandescence, finding
so little remains but reflection, glistening snail trails. Where we've been follows us like light.

Darkling I listen

Death is nature's remedy for all things. (Dickens) Death is only a launching into the region of the strange Untried; it is but the first salutation to the possibilities of the immense Remote,

the Wild, the Watery, the Unshored. (Melville) How I envy you death;/what could death bring,/more black, more set with sparks/to slay, to affright,/than the memory of those

first violets. (H. D.) I want Death to find me planting my cabbages, neither worrying about it nor the unfinished gardening. (Montaigne) ...not the worst that can happen to men. (Plato)

Death is hacking away at my address book and party lists. (Mason Cooley) The end of all stories is death, which is where time stops short. Sheherezade knew this, which is why

she kept on spinning another story out of the bowels of the last one, never coming to a point where she could say: "This is the end." Because it would have been. (Angela Carter)

The story-teller... has borrowed his authority from death. (Walter Benjamin) An old joke, but each individual encounters it anew. (Turgenev) Liberal hopefulness regards death as

a mere border to an improving picture. (William Empson) Death is not an event in life: we do not live to experience death. (Wittgenstein) Leave death to the professionals. (Graham Greene)

… is no more than passing from one room into another. But there's a difference for me, you know. Because in that other room I shall be able to see. (Helen Keller) The death... of

a beautiful woman, is unquestionably the most poetical topic in the world. (Edgar Allan Poe) Death unites as well as separates; it silences all paltry feeling. (Balzac) Suffering and fear are

born from the repression of the death wish. (Ionesco) Great is my envy of death whose curt hard sword carried her whom I called my life away; (Petrarch) Old age is life's parody, whereas death transforms life into a destiny: in a way it preserves it by giving it the absolute dimension... Death does away with time. (Simone De Beauvoir) ...the sound of distant thunder

at a picnic. (W. H. Auden) All societies on the verge of death are masculine. (Germaine Greer) The day of my birth, my death began its walk. It is walking toward me, without hurrying. (Cocteau)

Death hath had a thousand doors to let out life, I shall find one. (Philip Massinger) I know death hath ten thousand several doors/For men to take their exits. (John Webster) All good

biography, as all good fiction, comes down to the study of original sin, of our inherent disposition to choose death when we ought to choose life. (Rebecca West) When the body

sinks into death, the essence of man is revealed. Man is a knot, a web, a mesh into which relationships are tied... The body is an old crock that nobody will miss. (Saint-Exupéry) It's not

that I'm afraid to die, I just don't want to be there when it happens. (Woody Allen) There was one of two things I had a right to, liberty, or death; if I could not have one, I would take

the other; for no man should take me alive; (Harriet Tubman) Birth was the death of him. (Beckett) The sea is mother-death and she is a mighty female, the one who wins, the one who sucks

us all up. (Anne Sexton) And I thank my God for graciously granting me the opportunity... of learning that death is the key which unlocks the door to our true happiness. (Mozart) It was

a time when only the dead smiled, happy in their peace./Stars of Death stood over us,/and innocent Russia squirmed under the bloody boots. (Akhmatova) The call of death is

the call of love. Death can be sweet if we answer it in the affirmative, if we accept it as one of the great eternal forms of life and transformation. (Hermann Hesse) Darkling I listen;

and for many a time I have been half in love with easeful Death. (John Keats) The idea
of enemies is awful it makes one stop remembering eternity and the fear of death...

Possessions are the same as enemies only less so, they too make one forget eternity and
the fear of death. (Gertrude Stein) In every parting there is an image of death. (George Eliot) Death

is a master from Germany. (Celan) For them that think death's honesty / Won't fall upon them
naturally / Life sometimes / Must get lonely. (Bob Dylan) What do I know of man's destiny?

I could tell you more about radishes. (Beckett) ...a Dialogue between, / The Spirit and
the Dust. (Emily Dickinson) Death is terrifying, but it would be even more terrifying to find out

that you are going to live forever and never die. (Chekhov) Sport in the sense of a mass-
spectacle, with death to add to the underlying excitement, comes into existence when

a population has been drilled and regimented and depressed to such an extent that it needs
at least a vicarious participation in difficult feats of strength or skill or heroism in order to

sustain its waning life-sense. (Lewis Mumford) I need my little addiction to you. / I need that tiny
voice who, / even as I rise from the sea, / all woman, all there, / says kill me, kill me. / (Sexton)

The aims of life are the best defense against death. (Primo Levi) Being an old maid is like
death by drowning, a really delightful sensation after you cease to struggle. (Edna Ferber)

In the attempt to defeat death man has been inevitably obliged to defeat life. (Henry Miller)
At death, you break up: the bits that were you / Start speeding away from each other

for ever / With no one to see. (Philip Larkin) I used to think of death... like I suppose soldiers
think of it: it was a possible thing that I could well avoid by my skill. (Stendhal) And really,

the reason we think of death in celestial terms is that the visible firmament, especially at night (above our blacked-out Paris with the gaunt arches of its Boulevard Exelmans and

the ceaseless Alpine gurgle of desolate latrines), is the most adequate and ever-present symbol of that vast silent explosion. (Nabokov) Bullfighting is the only art in which the artist

is in danger of death. (Hemingway) You didn't feel there was anything you ever could enjoy again because you really were immersed in death. Other people seemed shallow. You felt

a strong allegiance to the dead. (Joan Furey, military nurse in Vietnam) Everything tends to make us believe that there exists a certain point of the mind at which life and death, the real and

the imagined, past and future, the communicable and the incommunicable, high and low, cease to be perceived as contradictions. (André Breton) As long as I have a want, I have a reason

for living. Satisfaction is death. (George Bernard Shaw) There is no such thing as inner peace. There is only nervousness or death. (Fran Lebowitz) ...the mother of beauty, mystical, / Within

whose burning bosom we devise / Our earthly mothers waiting, sleeplessly. (Wallace Stevens) Death can only be profitable: there's no need to eat, drink, pay taxes, offend people, and since

a person lies in a grave for hundreds or thousands of years, if you count it up the profit turns out to be enormous. (Chekhov) Do not speak like a death's-head, do not bid me remember

mine end. (Shakespeare) Death is the king of this world: 'tis his park / Where he breeds life to feed him. (George Eliot) No stout / Lesson showed how to chat with death. We brought / No brass

fortissimo, among our talents, / To holler down the lions in this air. (Gwendolyn Brooks) That's all the facts when you come to brass tacks: / Birth, and copulation, and death. (T.S. Eliot)

Auras

Opulent moonshine, ghost-glare and sheen, open the door to round luminance,
ovoid like the diaphragm, breath's base, air-side/dark-side, body/unseen.

Birthstone, pearl, globular quiet sheen, sound and its spherical echoes, mouth
of the hollow Green Dragon temple bell forged of bronze in Japan, pours out rings

of rung when struck by the log hung on a chain beside the bell beside the pond.
When my mother gave me the diamond ring that my father had given her at nineteen,

its band had been pounded into an ellipse, supposedly by thieves. The refugee jeweler
reshaped it to a circle, slightly too large, when I move my hand, a faint metallic clink.

Leopold Bloom loves sweet melons, buttocks, roundness in all forms except breasts,
a little too direct, face to face, his mind is acquisitive, fingering all impressions,

sights, voices, songs, newsprint passing by. In the Chinese scroll, color on silk,
"Scooping the moon from a golden basin," beside a window, full silver orb reflected

in water in gold. The Taj Mahal's long reflecting pool, designed with sides deeper
than center to reduce wave formation, called al Hawd al-Kawthar referring to

the "Tank of Abundance" promised to Muhammad. Telescopes used spherical mirrors,
but these suffered from spherical aberrations, so there's a shift towards parabolic

reflectors. Vermeer's "Woman holding a balance," the scale's empty pans reflect light
which also echoes the pearls, gold beads, the woman's domed belly, mirror on the wall,

her raised finger, the focal point from which all flows. When the ten sons of the Jade
Emperor were transformed into suns, they began to scorch the earth, so Houyi,

the immortal archer, shot down all but one, who became the sun we know. Enraged, the emperor sentenced Houyi and his wife Chang'e to live as mortals. Houyi sought

out the elixir of immortality for his sorrowing wife. Curious, Chang'e opened the box where it was hidden, drank it all, floating too high she arrived at the moon, where she

lives in the company of a jade rabbit. "Harvey and the Moonglows" formed in Louisville, first under the name "Crazy Sounds," reconfigured, the "New Moonglows" featured

the nineteen-year-old Marvin Gaye. Opalescence, out-bound or standing, weighing like a scale, the body's form inside, someone growing out of sight, making fullness,

as Brancusi's bronze "Bird before it flew" considers flight, the eye takes in the curve, bowl, swallowed, unborn matter. At dusk, the student archers roll their large white

targets in across the now dark field. Newly functioning, the Chinese lunar orbiter, Chang'e-1 began sending back photos of the moon's poles, adjusted its altitude

by two kilometers to avoid losing power during an eclipse. Nacre's hexagonal platelets of calcium carbonate crystals separated by laminae of elastic polymers,

chitin, lustrin, create interference with different wavelengths of light conveying iridescence, the mollusk entombs debris in this mother-of-pearl for as long as it lives.

Bioluminescence, light not generated by high temperature, dinoflagellates light up when they sense a predator of plankton through water motion, their brightness

draws larger predators who eat the first ones. Why the sky is blue—opalescent dichroism, highly dispersed. Up in the ionosphere, curtains or "quiet arcs,"

coronal rays in green and red, aurora's electromagnetic collisions of solar wind
plasma with earth's polar atmosphere, out in the magnetotail, light ions flowing.

In Aztec myth, the earth mother becomes pregnant, the child springs forth in armor
and slays his four hundred siblings, tosses his sister Coyolxauhqui's head into the sky,

her name means "face painted with bells." Pallid St. Elmo's fire in the yardarms, Darwin
on the *Beagle*, "Everything is in flames, —the sky with lightning, —the water with luminous

particles, and even the very masts are pointed with a blue flame," called "spirit candles"
by Welsh sailors, really plasma, an ionized gas with free electrons, like neon, seen on

leading edges of aircraft, cattle horns, the Hippodrome of Constantinople under siege.
Self-begotten Thoth, ibis-headed, crowned by crescent moon, Egyptian god of writing,

magic, science, who weighs the hearts of the dead in his scale gave Isis the words
to resurrect Osiris: he's a bird who lays a golden egg. Baboons are sacred to Thoth

because they sing under the moon, in the Ogdoad version, the cosmic egg is a gift from
Thoth, it hatches the four male-female pairs representing the forces—primordial water,

invisibility, darkness and eternity. Some think oxygen deprivation of the right angular
gyrus causes a near-death experience's commonly described aura of longed-for white light.

Vault

After being imprisoned in the Bastille, Arouet (missing only one vowel) changed his name
to Voltaire (R. Holmes, "Voltaire's Grin") echoing the name of the family chateau, Airvault,

which now hosts an annual didgeridoo festival, liking the associations with "voltige" (acrobatics
on horseback, later Voltigeurs, French military skirmish units created by Napoleon), "volte-face"

(a spinning about to face one's enemies), and "volatiles" (originally birds, butterflies or any winged
creature). His first poems were in alexandrines. On TV, svelte Olympians fly off the springboard

and over the vault, twisting, flipping in air, needing to stick the landing. We stayed in our friend's
small room, large enough only for bed and piano. He said to watch for the sleek long-tailed

creature that crawls in which he insisted on calling a vole. Vault cytoplasmic ribonucleoprotein,
a barrel-shaped organelle of eukaryotes, exhibits eight-fold symmetry, something to do with

nuclear pore complexes, transporting messenger RNA. Order, the mind likes it, make it mine,
mine the ore of language, tongue it through the mouth, out the rough pink trough, pronounce,

utter a list, save it on paper, book as bank vault: first bilingual dictionary—Mesopotamia,
cuneiform tablets, Sumarian words, Akkadian equivalents, 2300 BCE; Chinese lexicon in

the Shang Dynasty; Apollonius compiled a list of words used by Homer. If the change-up fools
the batter and he still connects, it will probably be a foul; the sonnet's volta, a change-up by

another name. At Wimbledon an unforeseen overthrow catapults the young Spaniard into
the royal box, while out on the far courts, dazzling, the oldest, Martina's inside-out backhand.

One love and then another had grandfathers who were revolutionaries—one Bolshevik friend
of Lenin's who left St. Petersburg in 1905, one fighting to bring down the Qing emperor, both

learned to make Molotov cocktails. In parkour, a not-quite-martial art, leaping as if escaping
an emergency, types of leaps include monkey-vault, lazy, underbar, tic-tac, you can see it on

YouTube. When two semicircular vaults intersect, they create a true ellipse, known as a groin.
In geometry, a Steinmetz solid is generated by the intersection of two cylinders, also called

mouhefanggai, Chinese for two square umbrellas. Crypt—a vault containing sarcophagi;
a church built over a cave, the mithraeum; a mystery religion, Mithra, the Persian sun god.

Pole-vaulter Stacy Dragila, gold medal in Sydney. Struggle between gravity and the desire for
thrust, aerious vs. going to ground. For the barrel vault or masonry arch each voussoir presses

against others to generate support, not complete until the keystone is in place. Playing behind
Chaplin, the incompetent Keystone Cops. To support a dome, pendentives, spandrels, Islamic

squinches, corbels, or the Chinese version the duogong, out-jutting like a beak, (not the sea cow,
dugong.) The wish for air-nature battling earth-nature, soil pulls, breath aspires, buttressed, both.

I

The terrible mind and how it wanders, automatic gestures,
a built-in push away from contact, or the eagerness to hold

like a heat-seeking missile, air to ground, flash of lightning
can rearrange your ventricles forever, just one bolt, never

the same. Standing around in the whereabouts of some
magnetic field, did you say "love"? Where do we go from here?

Waiting you've outlasted everyone. Lost gold or ashes? The sweep,
the arc, ocean's white light, web of sight, invisible intersecting

quanta of sun. Whatever it is is going too quickly, unraveled
like the ball of time, a free-fall mind, catch as catch can, the list,

recitations, the sovereignty of reason—how could you? Did you
really say that? To her regal face? Flip slip of the tongue

in its wishiness, the glitch, perfect error, fateful overlap of the said
with the truly meant splashes out to surprise. Inky squid,

clear cartilage, sauté with wine. On the platter she saw his heart
and penis, with two lungs arranged on the side, puffy and white

and she thought they should be honored, buried and thought
of the back yard, cedar-shade, hawthorn dropping its whiteness—

that would be the place—she looked at the plate again. Gone.
Then she felt an old-meatiness in her mouth, organ taste,

dried blood and thought, "I've eaten them," and the dream went on.
Here we go again, learning to excuse quite a lot, because we have to.

The precious engagement watch, gone, omega to alpha. Is that
a poached egg? Ab ovum over and over. Humbling, the fall into

a sack of bones, slack-jawed, chicken-necked, wrung. My mother
used to watch the chickens circle after the cook wrenched

their heads off, hence the saying as we always said. She never
learned to cook until we left, then, heaven upon a plate,

the ceramic discs growing larger and larger, like the necklace wars
perpetrated with her sister, the biggest beads, heavy and laden

with value. Once I watched her try on hollow hammered
golden ones the size of golf balls. No sale. Would she want

to be buried in them? Now everyone talks about their reflux.
Autoimmunity becomes you. Fortnight lilies reseeding themselves

at the curb. So easy to fly, it's falling really, falling with a bit
of horizontal glide thrown in, to give that illusion you love.

Genius of waiting, time runs infinite laps, you poise, pre-leap,
that swan-dive you never mastered. Try harder. Maybe wishes

can make your shoulders sprout a little something. You hover
at that volcanic rim where others take heart and leap into

some solidness you can't envision. Each toe wonders what it has
come home to, one mud, soles' tough pads scuffing the unlofty edge.

Pith

Light-hearted, I thought we'd jump together, my father held my hand, barnacled ladder,
weedy, high platform, saline green below. Go—I leapt alone, looked up to see the traitor

waving. I surrendered to our small channel of the hydrosphere, consanguine with larger
ocean, mermen dolphining over the rilled sea-floor, palace of the underwater king, we'd

go there. A father's heart, congenitally misshapen, bicuspid aortic valve scars with
time, aneurysmic root, strictured arteries, re-plumb the hole thing, implant a pig-valve,

still bleeding three days out, re-do the sonogram, sound the aquatic chambers, sonar
navigation, translation of sound to light / dark image, everyone keeps saying "We're not

out of the woods yet." Around the room of private conversation, an audible wall.
Within, beneath, indoors. Once I developed breasts, our hugs became side-long.

Withershins, against the sun, contrary to what's natural, trying to turn back the hands
of the clock, Harold Lloyd holding on for his life to the minute hand at IX. He'd lost

his thumb and one finger to the explosion of a prop, a supposed-to-be-fake live bomb.
Rough weave of afternoon's yellow, the too-bright stripes of seeing between slats,

are we as hungry as all that? Everything arranged for inattention, are you sorry we
came so far? Did you look both ways? Blinds because we live facing west, then flying so

far we arrived at East, living in circles, always a layer unseen. Pealed—what pours
through the skin of sound, boiled milk and its skin, skimmed and poured, pouring over

words out loud, ear's whorl, pore, background noise, envelope and paper knife, piercing,
dumb words on paper lifted by the tongue, belled into being, crossing over, nothing

into something. When I was a Three, in the hierarchy of Attending, Resident, Intern,
Sub-I or fourth year student, third year, the clinic's Attending introduced me with my new

stethoscope, to his oldest patient, on her Mayan face, a smile I couldn't fathom. Listening to
her brown chest wall, a far away galloping, too far, the doctor's swallowed-the-canary grin said—

go right—there—meaty red systoles, an inner world turned backwards, her secret, *mi madre*
something, maybe she'd had dextrocardia too. Found wild in the Maghreb, Ardi-Shoki,

ground-thorny thistle. "Artichoke Capitol of the World," now Castroville, features at its annual
festival Miss Artichoke and green ice cream, scoop out the choke-fuzz, heart-bound, folate-rich.

Earthshine. Around earth's solid metal core, a molten one. Inner core, densest in our solar
system, gold and platinum and other siderophilic elements, spins faster than the outer core.

In Biology, making a ventral slit up the belly of the slimy pithed frog, approaching its
three-chambered heart, some got queasy and the ones who loved looking got curious.

Our parents took us to see earthwork mounds, one sinuous snake 1200 feet long,
we rolled down the sides, lay in the grass looking up, pretending we could all lie down

together being buried here though seeing sky. Adena people, 6th c. BCE Ohioans, later,
the Fort Ancient culture added on, my brother found an arrowhead, or maybe a lithic core

we took for one, stony edges chipped off. In the same century the Adena were building
mounds, Homer sung his Odyssey, his hero visiting Kore, Iron Queen of the underworld,

and writing in Sanskrit, Sushruta described the circulation of the blood. In singing class
they taught us Stephen Foster songs, or "Green Cathedral" or "This land is your land,"

they tuned us to dead center, middle C. Then suddenly asunder, my father's work
transferred to Florida, gone—a hole in evening's fabric, lasting so long I was afraid

on return he'd blunder and throw out the bony new black kitten he'd not yet met. Finding
fossils beside the creek bed, he wanted me to understand the baking force that formed

them, packed mud layers in the dinosaurs' time, sediment encases, petrifaction, unfound
for eons, he cultivated wonder. Twenty one days after conception, human heart cells

begin their electrical beat, the four multi-leafleted valves of the heart were first described by
a Hippocratean. Ibn al-Nafis first observed the pulmonary circuit, where liquid blood-nature

becomes air-nature, transubstantiation. At cards, he always tried to shoot the moon, dog and
pup, "girl after my own heart," the crux of childhood wasn't boredom, but boredom bred

imagining. At the beach, over his eyelids he positioned the shells we called baby-cradles,
really slipper-shells, I think. With flashlight, orange and fist he demonstrated sun rise,

eclipse, the year, day, gist of time, the rise and fall, come and go, plundered child's heart,
easy to convince that science is the same as wisdom, love and gravity all one thing.

Space

Center of the universe, us? Worlds, no word among us, no fetters on the long reach
of suckered octopus arms, I cut them off, cuttlefish, in the skillet's wine, they all go

purple-black. Constellations rotating in inky sea, "Of the sun which is always in one
and the same place, there is neither setting nor rising." (Yajnavalkya, 9th c. BCE)

"On the Sizes and Distances of the Sun and Moon," (Aristarchus, 3rd c.) heliocentric,
observing tides, Seleucus of Seleucia, Babylonian astronomer proved Aristarchus,

later, Copernicus. Uncentered, free to reel and be particles, wave and mass vibrating,
strings, ocean-blanketed globe, spinning its way through smell-less blue-black. In space,

no petrichor, scent of rained-on earth, expansive endless vacuum, the mind can't contain
something without edges. Copper age, ten thousand years of smelting, Otzi, the iceman,

found in a glacier with copper-tipped axe, five millennia old, arsenic in hair from his work
in smelting copper whose symbol is that of Venus and the mirror, now the female sign,

we dig up that which shines, ductile metal, conducive to electron transfer. At lake races,
the rivalrous eighty-year-old women collect their medals in fake bronze and gold, one says

she has so many she hands them out for treats at Halloween. Trans-Tahoe relay, off the boat
into endless blue, translucent depths, sun rays penetrate and fade to vanishing point, clarity

and buoyancy—this is outer space, frightening, that look inside the cosmic mouth. "Finite but
unbounded," they said. Last things, a letter doodled upon and never sent, one call unreturned,

one call placed while looking out my office window, red-rimmed, manic, as if disbelieving
in his dying, I drew while he described his hospital room. "Gathering swallows twitter

in the skies"; "Faded the voice, warmth, whiteness, paradise—" (Keats) At twelve, going
with my best friend to our old elementary school at night, we climbed on the jungle-gym,

remembering when we were children. Sky-gazing, we saw a tiny light, pre-Sputnik era,
it's arc suddenly disrupted, it turned one sharp right-angle, then another, and continued on.

Moving from adolescent feeling of centrality into middle-aged sense, one of many,
peripheral, going to vanish while everything will continue to spin. Labor complete,

where's the golden fleece, the cup, the prize. There was supposed to be a grail and
they searched through primeval forests encountering mailed dragons, the black knight,

green-skinned maidens, but never found, except in a vision, the object of their quest.
Bottom of the well, look up, the ground tunnels down, water table, rabbit hole, looking

glass, netherworld, we revolve around dark, not sun. People died for heliocentrism.
The dead form the gravitational center of the underneath, magnetism, pull of matter

for itself, pulled to nothing. The novel (Calisher) where random humans on a space-
ship know their return mechanism has failed, outward bound, until food runs out,

the dramatic situation—to continue, die of cold, starve, suicide? Facing the void,
pencils and yellow pads, the saved peonies becoming crisp, dust motes dancing,

whirl of atoms, finite and bounded, leaps and swerves, heading out of bounds,
we're bound to go there beyond the edge of known space, dissolving, gone and timely.

Idyll

Iditarod, a thousand-plus miles to Nome across ice fields, mush!, a giddyup idiom said
to huskies; in a collision of sled dog and moose, the broken-leg dog flown to Anchorage

was afterwards fine. Here we go again, a tale told by… Poor Myshkin's seizures,
spasm of dark within dark, quixotic quest of the good for what it can rescue, idée fixe,

persnickety about light and its undoing, falling to the ground, a razing of consciousness,
time between the world and elsewhere, a diddling period, ungrounded by common

sense, the euphoric, transcendent otherwise, idealist "poor knight," white flight from
the tragedies of modern life. Testis to epididymis to vas deferens to out there, sperm

are unable to swim until mixed with fluid, spuming out in peristaltic waves of ejaculate—
idiot-proof, the process of becoming, unless an idiopathy intervenes, slide down, quick

clutch. In England they line them up in an identity parade. Who can remember who's
who? Were you you before you were born? The twins curled alongside, one pulse

became two, not quite knowing who's on what side of the line of I-ness, speaking
an idioglossic language, mother shut out, we two, free here, no sense of the outside

only the in, meaning diddlysquat to whoever might hear here. Dido, blasted by
a whirlwind for all time, funeral pyre burning the marriage bed, Aeneas gone to sea

again. Lost. The queen immolating and stabbing herself on his forgotten sword.
In utero, sound would be part of what holds and surrounds, hum and swoosh,

pulse and gurgles, noisy place, the womb. To cure colic, they swaddle, hold
up-side-down and to replicate a continuous rushing sound, a Dust-Buster will do.

Light before sound, or the other way around? Didgeridoo, the world's first wind
instrument, though the conch shell might argue, breath-course, lung-flute, tongue,

perhaps following ideophones, where the vibrating body of the instrument makes
sound, eg. percussion. Hornbostel-Sachs system has the conch as an aerophone, with

sub-numbers for lips being the only means of changing pitch. Didactic? Idiosyncratic,
this wish to sing and describe, sub-types, systems of usage, history of myth and

shell, blown skeleton, turquoise and coral, Tibetan emblem, Hindu shankha, voice going
into, under, chords reaching out into Himalayas' peaks and troughs. Olympic torch

making its bid there, among the rebel-monks, the faithful plowed under by the wide tide
of Han. Is this ideolect or mother tongue? Idi Amin titled himself Lord of All the Beasts

of the Earth and Fishes of the Seas and Conqueror of the British Empire in Africa in
General and Uganda in Particular. In tiddlywinks, a large disc called a squidger is used

to fire off the small winks, custom made, maybe plastic, rubber or onyx. Sit and play, so
little time, piddling it away, down elusive tubes, out the proverbial window, wider, open,

fetch until we can't, unanswerable riddle: "Why is a raven like a writing desk?" The Id
was really "it" until Strachey made it Greek, not quite wanting to leave it so naked,

the mind of the child so id-ridden, defining baby as "an alimentary tract with no sense
of responsibility at either end," id as source of libido, longing, that which does not hear

"No." Fiddlesticks, get rid of it. Wild, the boy's breath called "Idiot Wind." Hinting at
the terrible otherworld, Euripides' "Whom the gods would destroy, they first make mad"

might not be his, misattributed. Misled, drip by drip, water torture, good riddance to lost causes, hidden lungs, burrowing down into earth's middle, solid core, iron and nickel,

beneath a viscous mantle. At seventeen, arriving at Idlewild and finding the world larger than imagined, people more various, lost in the Alphabet Avenues, needle park, the poet's

white cat named Beauty, nidus of something, stray words, lost souls, cockroaches, time breeding unsolvent images, I fiddled while someone made sense. I did a lot.

Crystal Objects

Silver surface into which you dive, exploding liquid, you sink as droplets rise, oblique
pointy pearls fall back to pool, reflective layer viewed from underneath, what the eyes hold—

rippled mirror, what the lungs give out then long for—bright bubble, recurrent: catching one
of those escaping air-pockets, inhale, miracle, able to breathe underwater, exist as fish. Rainbow

scales accrete to themselves the eye, the oil slick, gunnels and floor boards, caught and fought
for over hours, landed, meaning fish removed from its native breathable element, hauled across

into ours, the boat imitating the fish will kill it, solution: release. Molecules float in solution
until they find each other and express their idea of shape, form occurs. Solids are crystalline

or amorphous, glass is a vitreous liquid. Skating on the little pond, so surprised when
my leg fell through to muddy bottom. Doing things with sound or light, crystals generate

a piezoelectric effect, jazzed molecules excited about themselves, Swarovski beads sewn into
the bodice of her wedding dress rhyme with her square diamond. Always asking what's inside,

the children loved the restaurant's transparent pyrex tea pots, leaves in sunken chamber, hole-
pierced, infusing bo lei from clear to brown to almost-black. Wanting to see inside the hive,

hexagons of honey where hidden pupae bees reside, the hymenoptera in chrysalis, an aurelian
is one who studies their emergence. The oldest lens, the Nimrud, dates back to Assyria, used

to start fire or magnify, lens from lentil. "Thus, what is mirrored can include what is visible
at the surface as well as what is not visible, disavowed, and even impossible. (In this usage,

the mirror becomes not a reflector but a kind of magical window.)" ("Lacan's Mirror Stage," J. Muller)
Hourglass, we measure what goes by in silicate granules, flip, and start again, at altitude the eggs

got underdone, we want them just half-soppy, you can still find eisenglass on-line for your potbelly stove, surrey curtains, boat. Looking inside is arriving underneath, backside of

the mirror, interior of archaic shape, netherworld of volume, H_2O, elemental substrate creates hexagons, the basic triad, one oxygen and its two surrounders, acts as template. At Yellowstone,

we arrived at Old Faithful just as a blizzard began, near white-out, saw the geyser blow, droplets spray up and out through thick masses of flakes, six-pointed needles, sectored plates, hollow

columns, spatial dendrites, rimed crystals and irregulars. In 1885 at the age of 19, Wilson Alwyn Bentley, made the world's first photomicrograph of a snow crystal in Jericho, Vermont. Long

considered odd, he caught it on a board painted black, held by wire "to keep away all animal warmth," was disbelieved for years, then the year his book came out, died of pneumonia caught

walking in a snowstorm. Film, "The Fall," slow grace, the elephant swims in turquoise water blowing silver bubbles from his trunk. Druids used beryllium for divination, or likewise water,

a scrying pool, or in Persia, the Cup of Jamshid containing the elixir of immortality in which one could see all seven heavens of the universe, or Palantír, Tolkein's Seeing Stone. Look into that

and find the self waiting in the future, vitreous shadow from the backs of the eyes. Lucretius's *On the Nature of Things,* six books in hexameter, describes matter made of particles made of minima,

time as parasite of matter in an infinite universe without a globe, events following from the wobbles of matter, and then there's a swerve—the leap out of mechanical causality into animal nature, free

will, a death in which the dead are dead. Mica's lustrous lamellae, sheets of silicate tetrahedrons, one theory— life arose on mica sheets in an oceanic earth, primordial soup, amino acids seeped between layers allowing long protein-chains, mineral birth-bed, powdered mica mixed with pigment used in earliest cave paintings. Looking into a hole in the ground left by a fallen tree,

in 1940, teenagers found the Caves of Lascaux and explored—Great Hall of the Bulls, 15,000 year old cattle multiplied before their eyes, Shaft of the Dead Man, now closed off to humans

whose breath formed enough calcite crystals to threaten millennia-old art. Lucretius described simulacra as quicksilver images that arrive in the eye, whirled off the surfaces of matter, air

sprouts images like soil yields grass. Prism hanging by a braided thread, cut glass edges break afternoon into rainbow elements, spins a little at the window, refracting rays rain light.

(Title is from Barbara Guest's "Belgravia.")

O

Reach into that thorny wicker basket. Not creation, only
a mood. Spit and you find… Start from the beginning, one

good turn, unlit days, spillage of work into night—it's always
turning, short day, long candle. Peculiar, wrapped inside

your surroundings so everything, linen drapes, grapefruit,
resembles the self, threads twisted and gnarly, raveled thought

where past and present merge, inseparable again as we always
wanted. Simple-minded, wanting something plain, not

flung prose, nothing browbeaten, another blank. One possible
polymer, knotted sticky molecule, organic. Is it time to eat?

Cat bathing beside the fallen nest, blue fragments of egg,
Indian summer desiccated the garden, rose bush with dark red

new stems. Feathered thoughts. Jump in bare, glacial lake,
liquid from the veins of no one, the beyond could reach in

and eat you, that fear again—prehistoric teeth, or the falling
boulder's molten force, or time which scares you most.

Lime tree yellowing. Did you forget your appointment?
Lost ones, speaking all day to the back of the mind.

"She's working your nerves, with her corkscrew nails and
violet eyes." Ah, this is the way—going where we have to go,

the pit, the bed, thread and bough, it rocks and breaks.
"Are you she? Tell me how to tell." Can't. Won't. "If you sit

with me inside the lizard's nest, I'll breathe. If you leave me
without the basket of bread, I'll die there." Crumbs, so little

to follow, the trail branched more than anyone could bear,
will we go there? "Time, so terrible, since I did not invent it."

Another day, "You forgot to answer the phone. Meant
to destroy me. Proves I don't exist." You wanted to go and

that meant being someone. Raised as mollusk, how to stand?
"I married chaos and you came to find me." Breathing

forms an inside, somewhere for the air to go means a body,
a body that breathes means a self. Collapse, retreat, "Is that

what words are for?" Seek and it happens, which way do you
tumble, up or down, you'd read that Alice liked tunnels, so

followed the nonsense as if unwound from the spool
of a primal place. The clock's lost wheel. *The Golden Key's* journey

to the center of earth. Ooblek, Puddleduck, Mulberry Street,
pool of needlessness, dive in. "No, you're water and there's

no one else." Swim again, little fish, you always loved the aquatic,
unfurl the small hand, candle-lit fingers, embryonic red glow.

Walking, breath and step, a metered going, inhale fog-air,
light ebbing, slippery eucalyptus leaves sliding out from under.

Hole

Worm holes, interconnection of the nine dimensions, space-time continuum gone holy,
hole in one, those heaps of worm dung, casings piled beside earth entry, going in,

cozy burrow, a home just the size for your body, facing out towards all predators and
escape. Channel between worlds, ring of the world, opening between in and out, border,

sphincter, that which wholly holds, muscular container, terrifying box. Dutch movie,
"The Vanishing," opens with a scenic drive through the Alps, then the little car dies

inside a tunnel, one small spot of light far at its end. Later, the girl goes missing and her
obsessed lover spends years searching, and finally receives a reply, "If you want to know

what happened to her, meet me etc.," and he goes to be caught by the claustrophobic killer
who chloroforms him, bundles him off, then he wakes, just as his she did, sealed in a coffin

underground. You wake and feel your immobility, breathless collapse, pound and scream,
crib where you cry and no one comes, night, wet, the sleepers never answer, you wait inside

the silence of the dead. Poe thinking nothing more beautiful than a young woman's corpse,
the story was—almost three, he's left alone with his mother's cold body. A form the mind

takes when built around the gone: sarcophagus, urn, encryption, corners of the self become
a tomb, vault, hard to take shape within a cloud-shadow. A ghost takes up space. In "The Dead"

when Gabriel learns that his wife loved a young man who died for love of her, the shape
of his life shatters, the thick glass that has held him cracks, lenses, window panes, reflections

on glint surface, finger tips on window, now the snow taps back from the netherworld,
dying he takes his first breath—grief breaks the shell of him. A golden watch polished

between fingers, embossed with leaves, winds down, the story reveals him to himself
as one of the dead. He hadn't thought to be among them quite so soon. "The snow was

general..." Commanding, commandeer, commedia, commando, commemorate, commend, commensal, commensurable, commence, no comment, commandment. We all follow orders,

time remands us, about to be scattered remains. She felt she died as a child when no one came in the night, when whoever held her seemed to have eyes of black mirror, soul of no one,

empty mummy wrap. Pyramid, primordial mound, built on the Nile's West bank, west as land of the dead (in China, the Western Isles.) They hid the central tomb down unclimbable shafts,

subterranean, oriented to earth's poles, the queen's chamber lower down, rooms laid out along the shape of the Eye of Horus, the ratios are half, 1/4, 1/32, 1/64 with 1/64 thrown away

equals one; half is smell, quarter sight, one eighth is thought, then hearing, taste, touch is smallest, also represented by a leaf or a leg on the ground, stands for rest and healing.

The dead don't answer, though they walk and breathe their earthy breath. Some wormholes are not considered traversable, their mouths held open by exotic matter, stuff with negative

mass/energy, going here to there through space/time sink holes, won't we all? There's a hole in your logic. You call this a hotel? The electron or the shortstop has left his position,

the surface has a pip where it vanishes, enter, emerge elsewhere, "This is the dream's navel, the spot where it reaches down in to the unknown." (Freud) Center of the belly, lost link, broken

cord, woven into otherness. From here we floated in outer space, cosmonauts of the abdomen, abandoned to air and earth, we miss music, the muscular hoofbeats, heart-surge fillings, gorged,

filled and fed, too large for nowhere, cave out, birth bed (he went in, you came out) central nest, red purse, humming meat, oven, stairway to otherwise, funnel, the necessary door.

Tongue

Oceanic mania, that peculiar elevation of expanse in tune with the vast ballooning
of internal energies which glow and spill over into excesses of verbiage without

shape, urge without object, me-ness without limit, no salt on the tail, centrifugal
and upwards. Did we go there? Syntax, syrinx, sex, sphinx. A single synapse,

when really, the axons and dendrites interconnect with delicate non-touch, tiny
chemical boats set sail in the dark cleft, unpacket themselves on the far shore

and memory occurs: a plum drops off the tree into your open palm. I loved "syrinx"
for its over-layered meanings: panpipes, a bird's vocal organ, narrow corridor of

an Egyptian tomb, a fluid-filled tubular cavity in the spinal cord as in syringomyelia.
Let's sing, because we can still walk upright like creatures of our kind, and go visit

the underground gallery's opening. Hieroglyphics in orange and blue, unlike
the alphabet, leave room for imagination's twists, interpretations, more so

pre-Rosetta stone. The grave/the song, so tight, entrance to the soul's hollow,
breath's music was hidden in the sigh, the full throat's echo, tube into innards,

pink tree, white cords, gristled chords, bellowing, breaching, the mythic white-whale
spree, not breech, backside first. Old ones naming what should be known, sewn seeds

of character, four short strokes in the calligrapher's horse, gallop out of the mouth
on a long low note then scatter, scat, that spoken note-speak of the jazzy-tongued.

Hoof-beats mean zebras, phoneme means sense, word means breath shaped into one
mouthful articulated by consonants, air/palate, genioglossus, pharyngoglossus,

papillae— sweet, sour, (adazzle) salty, bitter— narrow pharynx down into
darkness, bifurcation of breath and liquid, two routes to nowhere. What goes in,

comes out, utterance or nonsense, the owl and the pussycat, an articulate caterpillar,
the far wind, and black sails, the ones they forgot to change so he leapt off the cliff,

reading the signal of his son's death. Is the tongue a mother or a father? Muscular
utterance. Hamlet—"For murder, though it have no tongue, will speak with most

miraculous organ." Echolalia: a psychotic mimicry; coprolalia: shit-talk; glossolalia:
speaking in tongues, a fluent going on, un-understandable, channeled from the other

side, an automatic writing from the oral cavity. Anna O. babbling in sentences of
infinitives in four languages, had to be "relieved of her imaginative products daily,"

by Breuer, (*Studies in Hysteria*), she invented the name—"talking cure." What can
be spoken into the notch of an empty cloud? Body urging upward mind's intent,

play, reach into old time's root and rift, the swift footed tongue precedes all sense,
rosy, slippery creature of quirky purpose, threshold of fools' gold, song's wet floor.

Milk and Honey

Vibration in the throat, hexagons of honey, the wax, the comb, royal jelly, he thought
it would make him immortal, bronze spoon, expectation and sweetness. Heaven is a hive

of humming. Translucent wings, the bee-dance finding clover, lavender, orange trumpet
vines, scented seed homes, sex-havens called flowers, humdrum. The queen ovipositing

into six-sided cells, tended by nurse-bees, the mother looks away. Specialized mouth parts
form the architectural wax, spermatheca, the part within the queen where sperm is stored,

gathered in flight. Buzz-pollination: bumblebee alights on a petal and quivers, pollen
falls like snow, collects on hairs, groomed into leg-sacs; the larger the bee, the lower

the buzz. Super-organism, the collective life/mind of the hive. What's inside
the cardboard box? For me? The black cat lost her kittens because she hid them

so well, though she only had one at a time, a peculiar conception of "litter," almost
human. Humanly overlooked ovary, humble, center of something yellow, everyone

came through there once before time. Combustibles, those expressions of the future,
expectant or rinsing away. Corpus luteum erupting, egg's voyage, plump lining

at the ready. Unfertilized, gone, soon turns to ago, cells shedding. Bloody, those
expressions of the past: the noose, the guillotine, thumbscrew; now shackles and hoods,

waterboard, taser, same old human intent in sleek electric shape. More dead than anyone
counts, too bad lost souls can't power the grid, also humming. People kept changing

the labels honey bee, yellow jacket, hornet, wasp, bumble bee, so I never knew when
we meant the mean yellow ones and when the big furry black ones. In the orchard under

my grandfather's apples, late summer, 3, I learned how the insect guts pull out with
the stinger: flick it away, bee dies, father bending down. Still speaking at the open door,

hallowed absence where memory collided with the center of a self. Was there room
for a new baby? Did she eat it? The hamsters did, babies red as pistachios, my mother

told me not to mention the pregnant neighbor's stomach when she came to visit and
on arrival I immediately blurted, "How'd that get in there?" Because the lineage ended

with me, I was sure I'd killed the others. If a mouse wanders into a hive, it gets
embalmed in amber, sits mummified like furniture. That stupid repeating line about

"bit by a dead bee," Lauren Bacall answers in her smart way. Why was it only birds
and bees? Drones waiting to mate, the queen is fecund, fed by attendants, egg laying

busyness, twin desires, for life and murder. My mother, during the attorney general
hearings, says she thinks maybe torture is a good idea: "I'd do anything to anyone if

it saved the lives of my babies," like her baby, my brother, the grandfather. We argue
on New Year's Day, "You just have clouds in your head." She wants to believe

you kill off the bad and then we'll be safe forever. Rummaging in the bathroom closet
I found her diaphragm. Walking down the hall I held the mirror to look at the ceiling

and bewilder myself. Hard to realize they were my feet, my shoes, inside that illusion
of being slippered. I gave what space I owned. No, I took everything there was, sex

and sweetness, in Florida we bought orange blossom honey, the honeysuckle dies.
When asked my mother answered, "Breast feeding was out of fashion at the time."

Oracle

Put out to pasture—stretch out, gallop, nuzzle, side-flop down into clover and semi-wild pastoral greenery, alternate to the glue-factory. The chase is over, that hysterical relation

to desire, drop the handkerchief and expect to be pursued. Lily of the valley, tiny bell smell, the snail leaf curl in dark corners, ferny, thrilling tendrils of something. Riding in the car

from Ohio to Florida he taught us songs like "Off we go into the wild blue yonder... hell of a roar... flames from under." I thought about "blue yonder." Alphabet game in the car, always stuck

at Z or Q, happy to find the now defunct Quaker Oats sign. Pondering the passage of ads. We spelled for entertainment, tracking something that made sense from inside the Ford that

did not, following the humidity from valley to Gulf, trail of bread crumbs, rose petals, bridal path, the bed, potpourri in all her drawers, the bathroom, lavender water, lime oil. The sea turtle follows

her nose to Japan, recognizes her birth-beach by smell arriving 12,000 km from Baja, only to be snagged by a fishing net, drowned, tracked by GPS, wide swath of the globe, "at loggerheads,"

turtle, carved on the jade plaque, as emblem of longevity, eaten at the 80th birthday. "In the next ten days there will be no disaster." (translation from oracle bones) Shang dynasty, tortoise shell

heated, the cracks then read and inscribed. But the borders were besieged from the west so there was disaster after all. No pasture free from it, chewing the cud, ruminating, spacey, musing.

Sit and crawl, the leek, a soup, dinner not served but the ladle's ready, the blue dragon bowls and the white bakelite spoons. Spoon to lip to gullet to belly to bladder to bowl to bay. He simmered

the beef bones all day, pomelo peel, ginger, this will beef you up, add meat to your bones, fill out, bulk up, amplify. They sold the prize heifers by the pound, so exercise was tricky, wanting muscle

built and needing lard's heft, do you gallop or sit still? We'd drive to Lexington to look at horse
farms, the statue of Man 'O War. What were we supposed to do here? They said "bluegrass"

but it looked green to me. "Stud farm" offered food for thought, the future involved reproduction
which was carefully explained at school. Colts galloping out of exuberance, the male horse peeing,

mares sunning glossy flanks, foals walking on stilts as soon as they're out, teetering, wobble
towards that larger bulk, the mare. Pyromancy goes back six thousand years, you had to be

royalty for them to read the bones for you, applying a hot instrument to the turtle shell or ox
scapula, decipher cracks as omens, calligraphy of the unknown, power to the reader, bronze age

language, onomatopoetic or pictographic, or "phonetic loan" where meaning is acquired by
sound association, the important thing to communicate was that which no one knew. Yonder =

yawn + wonder, you + under. Future tense, what's auspicious, worrying about protection, about
home, your own acre, sling, nook, valley, safe and sound, grazing, nibbling the wild green now.

U

Inhabit the soft inner body, the yoga teacher says. Prime,
full sun radiating, the flat wide light of bronzy noon. Quiver

before the opening, there must be shadows on the other side.
The body wanted more and here comes less. Soaked seed

swells up sends its tendrils down into loam, loose humus crumbs
of earth holding, embryonic plant unfurls, sends out root-hairs,

assumes verticality, cotyledon splays itself to catch the full rays.
At yoga, sun salute, some of the old ones can't quite touch their

foreheads to their knees. Story of a stone—Parthenon Marbles—
usurped, dismantled across centuries: "Amphitrite, consort

of Poseidon, served as his charioteer. As a sea deity, she was shown
as a serpent. One of Amphitrite's arms is shown in a show-case

in an adjoining room." Shoulder asana, the feet refusing to stand
vertically. The question of mass is unresolved, measurement of circles,

six looping hours, five invisible atoms, our wish—calm undulating seas
and a prosperous voyage, flat ocean, gun-metal gray in all directions.

Varanasi, body chunks and ash mix with muddy water, air
is thick with smells, incense, burnt flesh, charring the lungs

of the living, children swim around the new yellow water-tower,
two stories tall, painted with a fat blue Vishnu. Leaf-cupped flowers

hold small flames, float down the Ganges, fragile offerings
of something beautiful, burn a few minutes then become part

of everything. Is *Man o' War* a ship, a horse or a jelly fish?
She'd swab our welts with turpentine when we'd stepped

on the alarming blue stingers. Left in too much sun upon
a yellow beach, nose scabbed, burnt, then bubbled.

Child's pose, Krishna said: "The Atma acquires a childhood
body, and an old age body during this life, similarly Atma

acquires another body after death." Over-full, the empty
hour, crowded in on by claims, fire-dreams, chimes,

predicaments of others. Vacation—over-designed wood
houses litter the coastal meadow. Occupy postures: warrior 2,

the bow, cow face, corpse pose. Sink into the floor. "Athena was
shown springing away from the centre of the composition...

her aegis, a goatskin garment with a fringe of snakes.
A fragment of her helmeted head is in Athens."

World of sun, the fuel that keeps things going, though
its life is finite too (in the billions, but still it dies). Soften

the belly, the gaze. No open space in the mind, a sea
clogged with debris, wrong words, slant images, a balloon

floating away, grinning cat, bouldery beach, warm oranges.
No reach, no heft. "The lapith was rendered in such

high relief that the carving has broken free and is now lost.
A drawing (1674) shows the missing lapith...warding the centaur

off with his right arm. The centaur's head is in Würzburg." Legs like
stone, immovable force meets hollow breath, flesh going its own way,

all descent from here, undulating flight, wobbly tree pose, a fight with
gravity, lost monuments, on the move, fine, this battered tin kettle of fish.

(Quotes are from the text displayed with the Parthenon Marbles,
The British Museum, London)

Refuge

The muscular tongue, hidden gullet, red, rugated, acidic, swallows, disappears, runnels
reabsorbed, the body becomes the body, have you eaten? Rosy tongue, urgency, down

is towards the you that is hollow, inverted pocket, hello? hungry? She locked the children
up, unfed and found at 19, he was less than 4 feet tall and 40 pounds. Someone studying

the language of feral children. Under-weavings of the weftless intertwined, tangled up
and unraveled, the cats bat the balls of colored wool around the living room ensnaring

the chair legs, plant basket, each other, roundabout, wound a bit. The tiger cub raised in
a New York City apartment eventually grew wily enough to plan, and when his owner who

had moved out came by one day to throw in meat, the tiger pounced. At the zoo, volunteers
arrive with bottles of sweet condensed milk, the elderly rescue-lion comes forward for his treat.

In the wild, he wouldn't have lived to nineteen. I forgot to open the gate across the driveway,
and the morning's first patient was locked out, phoned after awhile and I opened, her dream

the next day—one eye lid is infected, swollen shut. Nowhere is where we lived until someone
brought lunch. Tin bucket, luckless, tough lettuce, rough-house, roughage is good for you,

fiber holds the strings together so we don't fly apart, antimatter, such asymmetry, where is it,
the dark stuff? Water surface, silvered refractions, ripplings are the troughs of vision, see-through,

history marching in two directions on a flat screen, saris go one way, umbrellas the other.
The politics of being dead: my grandfather's third wife wanted the plot beside him, so had

my mother's mother dug up and relocated to a plot at the far edge. My step-father's coffin rested
on a metal contraption, hovering above the hole which was mostly concealed by Astroturf which

also concealed his first wife's grave, not pressing the fact that my mourning mother will not lie next to him, but will take the position of the far-flung other wife. The visible universe

unpeeling itself like a tangerine, easy, one shell, shelf, shall we go then? In Ozu's *Late Spring*, the father peels an apple his daughter used to peel for him, the skin dangles, holds the spiral—

whole—then severed, falls. The ileum, the last two meters of the small intestines, is joined in the embryo to the umbilicus. In some, this duct fails to close before birth, called Meckel's

diverticulum, intestinal torsion may occur, or volvulus, the spiral cuts off blood and so, ischemia, a bit of gut dies. We think this caused my irascible father-in-law's colostomy. Kwashiorkor,

protein malnutrition, the big-bellied children; marasmus, calorie starvation, those who seem all ribs. As the unfed body becomes catabolic, it begins to digest all muscle, even the heart.

(800 million are undernourished, 20,000 die each day from lack of food.) "What a pregnant lesson to us is this prophet! What a noble thing is that canticle in the fish's belly! How billow-like and

boisterously grand!" (Mellville) Thrown off the ship for causing a huge storm, Jonah is delivered to the mouth, refuge from tumultuous waves, safety vault, whale-mother gestating, held for

three days. Earlier a sailor falls into the whale tied ship-side, so Queequeg dives in, becomes the obstetrician, skillfully delivers the lost sailor breech, back to life's salty, slick, unsafe surface.

After dark, hiking down from Mt. Tam, our headlamps bounced light off some reflective circle. Trail marker? It moved. Then, close enough to see the tail, to recognize wild eyes' opalescent

backs, we froze. The mountain lion glared, watched, we raised our hiking poles to look large, clanged them together, then a rush of leaves as the creature vanished into the underbrush and

our hearts resumed their quiet ways. Breath moving in and out of the chest's cave, springy,
how the sternum rises after chest compressions. Heart stopped, someone took charge and

shooed the relatives out into the hallway, I the intern, using the brute force of arms before
the cart comes carrying the electricity, voltage, IV's in soft plastic tubes, dropped syringes,

I heard the ribs crack, knew I'd broken them, hoping nothing punctured. The green screen
had a line with a few blips, S-T complexes, afterwards on rounds she said she felt she watched,

looking down from a corner of the room, hovering as in flying dreams, wingless, effortful,
then was pulled back into the body's core, care of others' hands, on white sheets, her cells.

Pacific Storm

Hydroplane, left lane, Bay Bridge, zooming through space, white puffs of cirrus fog, raining sideways, near-gale-force wind, cars struggle to stay within the white lines.

Out from under, we didn't cross the Styx like this, by FasTrak. Ferryman, boat man, barge-song, Whitman's crossing below the bridge, birds mew and reel, the gyre's

got us by the under-feathers, we scream like gulls. Did you lay an egg? The probability of earth over and over again, I wanted ash but he thought otherwise. In Marin

somewhere, an eco-cemetery, hole in the ground under a tree, no lawn, no path, boxless, wrapped in nothing or a cloth, muslin, sailcloth, three sheets to the wind,

(tipsy was "one sheet in the wind's eye"), rain seeping into us, loam and clay. Earthworms emerge on the pavement after rain, having tried to escape subterranean flooding, unable

to repenetrate the ground, they die. A group of moles, called a labor, squeezes the worm before eating to empty its guts of earth. To mate, worms overlap their front ventral surfaces

and exchange sperm, secrete a cocoon, back out of the tube and inject their own eggs and the other's sperm into it. Vermicompost is the richest manure. Formative minerals, baked

substance of all being, this hole is our house, I hold you here, soaking, falling, fallen. Eve took a bite, teeth, the slug-tongue, one ovary to another, passing through and emerging

from the other end, seed transformed by the bird who swallows, invisible worm, consuming the remains of the visible. We breathed inside that skin, then crossed, mouth opens and a pip

pops out, spit on the soggy ground—sprout, sprig, twig, leaf, petal and pip. We didn't dig in, we flew, the bridge held us on its black macadam bed, resonance collapsing

the Tacoma Narrows Bridge, Inca slung rope bridges, road-bed suspension invented in Tibet, humans in relation to spatial situations, ravine, river, cleft, chasm, wanting across.

Swimming in the race underneath the Gate, looking up at the orange South tower, avoid
the eddy around it, mouth full of bottle-green water, salt waves in the drink. On top,

we didn't sleep, we slid, sloshing through, we still have legs. I bought a small umbrella
at the Natural History Museum on a dark, about-to-pour day and walked across to

Broadway before I had to unfurl it, surprised to find a large gray dinosaur skeleton
filling the circle I'd expected to be all-black. The darkling beetle of the Namib Desert

collects water from fog condensing on the elytra. The glyph, a scarab, meant "to come
into being, to transform," the dung beetle was thought to exist only in the male form,

the idea was he injected sperm into a ball of dung and out came larvae, autochthony,
that dream of self-creation, fathered-forth. Spontaneous generation, one of the first

experiments ever, Francesco Redi, 1668, physician-poet put meat into flasks, only
the unsealed ones bore maggots. Something out of nothing, someone out of me, me out

of her, her out of the garden, awareness out of apple, beetle out of dung, word out of
scarab, seedlings out of rain. Early morning in Taiwan, the ox-cart comes to collect

night-soil in large buckets, used for fertilizer, transmission route for ascariasis, the children
pooping, squat and compare their worms. Our yellow hills go green this time of year,

three fronts of weather brought five feet of snow to the high Sierra, reservoirs half-empty still,
fog-blinded drivers bumping up against the probability of matter's equal and opposite

reactions, ceilings leak, mud slides begin, dinner in the dark, bedding down by headlight,
a gray moth finds us beside the sliding door, small globes of rain reflecting not much light.

Mud

My writing is as clear as mud, but mud settles and clear streams run on and disappear. (Gertrude Stein)
'Yes, and her petticoat; I hope you saw her petticoat, six inches deep in mud, I am absolutely

certain, and the gown which had been let down to hide it not doing its office.' (Jane Austen)
I'm a dirt person. I trust the dirt. I don't trust diamonds and gold. (Eartha Kitt) The young women,

who envied Anna and had long been weary of hearing her called virtuous, rejoiced at the
fulfillment of their predictions... They were already making ready handfuls of mud to fling at her

when the right moment arrived. (Tolstoy) Just now, at all events, he was only a pleasant weather-
washed wind-battered Briton, who brought in from a struggle with the elements that he

appeared quite to have enjoyed, a certain amount of un-removed mud and an unusual quantity
of easy expression. (Henry James) Sea horses floundering in the slimy mud, / Tossed up their heads,

and dashed the ooze about them. (John Dryden) A man should examine for himself the great piles
of superimposed strata, and watch the rivulets bringing down mud, and the waves wearing away

the sea-cliffs, in order to comprehend something about the duration of past time, the monuments of
which we see all around us. (Darwin) Her quickened step will be heard by the frogs in their mansions

of mud, and the fish, recluses in rayless pools, will rise to the light she brings. (Marian Storm) As the
pyroclastic explosion ran down the mountain, it became a driving force of boiling mud and heavy

moisture, reaching Herculaneum four minutes afterwards, colliding with the buildings at 400°
Celcius, causing the sea to boil intensely. (Arcane History) By avarice and selfishness, and a groveling

habit, from which none of us is free, of regarding the soil as property, the landscape is deformed,
husbandry is degraded with us, and the farmer leads the meanest of lives. He knows Nature but

as a robber. (Thoreau) Who made all things good which He created, He began the creation of man from clay. (Qur'an 32:7) We might say that the earth has the spirit of growth; that its flesh is

the soil. (Leonardo da Vinci) Unless a creature has bones or other hard parts, unless it wears a shell or is big enough and heavy enough to make characteristic footprints and trails in mud, it is unlikely

to leave any fossilized traces of its existence behind. (H. G. Wells) And I would liken her to one of those wild torrents which, when angry, overflow the plains, sweep away trees and houses, and carry off soil

from one bank to throw it down upon the other. (Machiavelli) He is rather like the great mosque of Dejenné, a magnificent structure made out of mud. (S. Greenblatt) We like March, / his shoes are

purple, / He is new and high; / Makes he mud for dog and peddler, / Makes the forest dry; (Dickinson) The poor woman had indeed been loading her heart with foul language for some time, and now

it scoured out of her mouth, as filth doth from a mud-cart, when the board which confines it is removed. (Henry Fielding) Dirt's a lot more fun when you add water! (Dennis The Menace) The tortoise

is very fond of water, drinking large quantities, and wallowing in the mud. (Darwin) The other horses too were frightened, and splashing through the water with their hobbled legs, and drawing

their hoofs out of the thick mud with a squelching sound, they bounded out of the marsh. (Tolstoy) Winds sweeping the level waters, can bear off a mighty part of wet, since we behold in a single night

the highways dried by winds, and soft mud crusted o'er at dawn. (Lucretius) The Moon-goddess Heqet was active in this creative work of the Potter-god. A certain hieroglyphic shows this goddess in frog-form.

She is associated with the swamp where the potter found his clay. One is led to suspect that the infants were created in pots. (H. S. Darlington) "The mud of Paris," thought he drowsily—for he now felt pretty well convinced that he would have to put up with the kennel as a bed—"has a most potent stink. It must contain a large amount of volatile and nitric acids, which is also the opinion of…the alchemists."

(Victor Hugo) We could only go down during a freshet; for the Little Missouri, like most plains' rivers, is usually either a dwindling streamlet, a mere slender thread of sluggish water, or else

a boiling, muddy torrent, running over a bed of shifting quicksand, that neither man nor beast can cross. (Teddy Roosevelt) But nearly all authorities are agreed [life] probably began upon mud

or sand in warm sunlit shallow brackish water, and that it spread up the beaches to the intertidal lines and out to the open waters. (H. G. Wells) The shortening days & the deepening mud have been

at the bottom of this affair. (Henry James) In Queensland it is believed that a part of the child's spirit (cho-i) stays in the afterbirth. When Anjea, the being who causes conception in women by putting

mud babies into their wombs, comes along and sees the place [where the afterbirth is buried], he carries it away to one of his haunts, such as a tree, a hole in a rock, or a lagoon where it may remain

for years. (James Frazer) The nest is placed in the most exposed situations, as on the top of a post, a bare rock, or on a cactus. It is composed of mud and bits of straw, and has strong thick walls:

in shape it precisely resembles an oven, or depressed beehive. (Darwin, about the oven-bird of La Plata.) "Look at that dirty child," he would sometimes say, with a cross glance at me; "it seems as if the young

rascal must go and stick himself into all the old plaster and mud holes he can find, he always looks so ugly and dirty." (Alfred de Musset) If you want me again, look for me under your boot-soles. (Whitman)

Worth

In Kenya, when they failed to buy beef for the army, the soldiers discovered elephant
to be both cheap and plentiful. Fort Knox, paradigmatic vault of gold. Now in the

Indonesian pit-mine, it takes 250 tons of dirt to find one wedding band's worth of gold.
Sifting, sieve and grid, cheese-cloth, mesh, the little silver strainer for our multitude of used

tea leaves, waste, we sip and rinse them down, lips to gullet to belly to blood, transit of
molecular blessings, Taiwan mountains to sun-splayed twigs to cup, cycles of intake and

wash, output and rinse, wave and tides under the moon's say-so. Pulse is what's permanent,
I'm waiting for them to find remnants of a cosmic death that must have preceded the big bang

that would have followed the previous birth and expansion before involution and collapse.
Elapsing, we wish we could remember what we meant to write this morning. It was as

wonderful as plums in the fridge. We bought a new energy-efficient one with freezer
drawer where the chewy Cheeseboard coop's bread sits and waits for us to want it.

My mother on the Inauguration's poem: It was all words. Worth goes back to Sanskrit's
vartate, "he turns," to and from every season, unto all that pours forth, pennyworths,

a little for me, a little for you. We're all having to do with less as the era of muchness
evaporates, what are we left with?—a house the bank owns, the view from here,

a few children's things—pennywhistle, leotard, sparkly valentine, Chinese picture-
books. The saved things reside in the upstairs closet, small cedar-scented wooden

hold under sloped ceiling. "Dreams, books are each a world." (Wordsworth) Years
elapsed, now the girls have grown, far flung. The elderly are leaving us, they turn

to hospice for help with beds and not walking, or for being unable to hold the spoon,
or to utter words, no more taking a turn around the park full of small houses for Ohio

bluebirds. We visit once more before he dies, on return, the milk in the fridge
has turned sour, we turn a blind eye, or nose, and feed it to the cats. When I kissed

my step-father goodbye, he cried, then shook his fists like an angry child whose words
no longer work, protesting what? his fate, my going, my making him cry? I said

Goodnight. Aphasia leaves him with the shape of a thought, but no language it can
fit inside of, frustration still here, but so cut off, he's become expert at commenting

with the lift of one eyebrow. Lunar New Year, those younger phone us for bai leen,
saying *Gung Hay,* we phone the older ones, Hong Kong, Taiwan, his 90-year-old amah,

new moon holding it's blackness towards us, the lit side said to resemble a white rabbit
looks away, the rabbit ears reside between what others see as sad blue eyes. The kelp-

filled sea, hidden otters, one with a baby on her belly, floating looking skyward, flips
herself over with a turn of the tail, down under, what comes up, nose first, oxygen

infill, return to sea-surface, a blighted beauty, pocked like the moon by comings,
goings, craters, silvered runnels, worth forging itself into form, the green-black waves.

Sometimes Y

Exchange, air-sacs, gill-rakes claim the needed element
from what surrounds, the nothing that feeds. An invisible yes.

The unseen, that's your mother who named you. Lost
feet, webbed limbs, swimming and flailing, breath

that could hold, too frail. Breath doesn't hold but
passes through, sustaining zephyr, a young minute,

next to nothing, one membrane, no knot but a film,
sliding the fleet and the viscous. Past solstice, reddening sky,

frost in the shade, which never happens here, phone-call,
hear of an acquaintance dead at 58, knee surgery, embolus,

end. He didn't know how little of the year he'd see.
Barely light, your breath pulsing, wavelets, the mornings

left, how many? As you were, at home in the galaxy's
long arm, spiraled off to a far corner, mysterious.

A long black veil, star's aura pierced by light,
the whorl of universe, nebulae, milky, in Chinese

myth it's the Silver River. His hoarse old voice failing,
miles to Mexico, did you ever go there when the jacaranda

trees flower? He said purple, purple. The eyes you wanted,
the robe, a voice that issues out of nowhere, sibyl's song,

groan, shriek, she fell backwards and the words came
forward, traveling in opposite directions, body rifts,

voice and echo, teeth and tongue, heart and pipes, guts
and spleen, lobed pairs. You forgot everything you had

helped to remember, all that arose you killed unkindly.
After all the mourners leave, hymns done, incense smoking

from the grave, leaves flapping, blacking in the rattling air,
eat, you know you're hungry, you know the wings are only

folded. Red papillae taste the air, the sea, the ever after,
yesterday afternoon's flat reach, no suddenness, the dream—

six dead, you can't name them. Her voice wasn't right,
you wanted that "Oh," gone. Wherever it goes—

the nothing no one knows. Black oolong, orangey scent
of elsewhere. Found at the bottom of the sea, blue on white

Ming porcelain beside the bones of some young woman, cook?
slave? sunk inside the ship's hold, all those treasures auctioned off

on e-bay, bid for an ancient teacup to sit beside the egg-yolk
yellow vase, after all those centuries below, let's drink.

Spell

Spelling was beyond me, "unlettered small-knowing soul," ungoverned, on
Sesame Street—Forgetful Jones. Hymns have their rhythm, Dickinson stole from

church, problematic anthems, black and white speckles on the "theme" notebooks,
blue lines, red margin. I ought to have a scheme, something other than a compulsion

to fill in the blanks. This is your skin, prepared for a thousand words, this is your
tongue prepared for four scrolls. "Certain bounds hold against chaos." (Robert Duncan)

Boundary, bondage, I'll take badinage, liking leaps and bounds without falls, no
bandages, two lines around white space makes a sandwich. Let's collage what

we can, form fractured and repaired, blend of is and isn't. What anchors? Shape.
What reflects? He skipped the flat rock four times, mine always sank: this was my

idea of the difference between genders; a brother is a terrible thing to confuse.
We asked questions, nothing was spelled out. We'd wind colored balls of yarn

for our ancient great-aunt's basket of red, yellow, purple guarded by her wiry
little dog, Mr. Dooley, while dwelling upstairs my psychotic uncle mumbled and

chomped his teeth. Woolgathering, I find myself humming and think of him. The bee,
I'd drop out early, sit and watch others' effortful tongues and cheeks, eye scrunches,

as if the face could help the mind remember what it never knew, deduce from root
and elemental codes, (logorrheic, gluttonous, fieriness, gelastic) whoever knew

won a giant Hershey bar. A machine taught speed-reading, phrases clanked
by in threes, waltz time, the more they pushed, the more I dawdled, held

the words in my mouth, refused to let my eyes get ahead of my body. A hexagram
predicts the future, a hex holds you, a painted sign on the barn door keeps cattle safe,

hexachlorophene in toothpaste ads. Spelunking sounded so alarming, scaling those
vertical tight chimneys, caverns where air has never been, bats and piles of guano,

people got stuck. Those stupid tourist caves they took us to, colored lights on
stalagmites (Witch's Finger, Carlsbad Caverns), drip formations, time as sculptor,

mineral as material, car trips, boredom beyond reason, singing helped but more,
we wanted out. "Eye of newt... adder's fork... lizard's leg... like a hell-broth boil

and bubble." It came in a dream, the structure of the hexane ring, when Kekulé
saw the ouroboros, double carbon bonds create a form, and along comes a smell.

In "Spellbound," Gregory Peck thinks he's a psychiatrist but learns otherwise,
anxious about black lines on white, ski tracks in snow, forgotten murder of his brother,

all that repression undone by Ingrid Bergman, undoing herself along the way. Line
gives way to consciousness, Plato's circular creature as first in the universe, one

who consumes its own shit, self-feeding, dawn of being, undifferentiated pre-shape
as circle, thought as line of black on white, letters marking the tongue's moves,

lovely chocolaty aftertaste, palate, pharyngeal pillars, taste's papillae, teeth and throat,
modulating form and breath out of dark mucosal space, sound's palette, must we speak?

Fire

In breath, out-take, trachea, bronchi, heart-sac, the great vessels, down there curled
up with the lungs' alveoli, internal combustion produces heat and light, chain

reactions. Each cell generates quiet energy, thermal goings-on, hot-headed, warm-
blooded, boiling water, swoon and roilings, romance of the over-done, half-baked,

incendiary. Pele, goddess of dance, volcanoes, lightning, violence, dug her o'o into
the earth, but knew the goddess of the sea would flood her home, so moved uphill

to Mauna Loa, a cliff dedicated to her brother, the king of sharks and of the gourd
that holds life's water used to revive the dead. Zoroastrian fire festivals celebrate

purity, healing, truth. Playing with fire, Zeus chose the bone wrapped inside fat
and not the meat hidden inside stomach lining, so what looks good and isn't

became the sacrificial offering. Monks immolating themselves to end the war.
Flame, exo-thermic, self-sustaining, only partly plasma, emission spectra include

black-body radiation of soot and infra-red bands. White is the hottest, then yellow
then red, the uncombusted rising in black smoke. At the burning ghats, when

flame meets the organs, the belly opens its contents in yellow-black smoke, we breathe
meat smell, congesting our lungs with those of the newly departed. Fire, lightning,

sun, all one thing to the Vedic god. Prometheus gave us fire, and in retaliation, Zeus
sent Pandora, first woman, molded out of earth, with her jar of greed, envy, longing.

Fire's role in evolution—early humans learned to cook, widened their spectrum
of nutrients, consuming meat led to larger brain-cases, The Cradle of Humankind site,

northwest of Johannesburg, shows evidence of the hominid Australopithecus's control
of fire for over a million years. Warfare—those inside the Trojan horse set fire to Troy.

Spark of the synapse, imagination/memory, too-muchness—Kajuraho's erotic carvings,
Keats coughing up blood, the splay of mycoplasma, no oases, caravan in the sand,

one hump or two, the camel grins, cigarette packs we decorated with wavy psychedelic
lines of orange and purple, grousing, blue pheasant beating its breast in the evening,

colonnades at temples, Shiva lingam, at Angkor Wat banyan tree roots consuming
the temples, holding the architecture, dissolving. We brought flowers and incense

floating off on a petal, one tiny candle, smoke and ash. Inside the lion, intestinal villi:
outside the villa, two lions guarding the gate with serious smiles. The body is the mind,

glass and pinkness, the ballerina whirling on top of the music box, she doesn't eat so
she has no insides, only muscle and will and the four-fingered grace of position, little girls

in tulle (actually bobbinet, in which winding the weft around the warp thread creates
hexagons) pliéd until we hurt, the teacher wiped my brow saying "That's what I like!"

Ricochet is practical in billiards, less so with thought. Rickshaws fitting just between
the ancient stone walls of the temple and the tourist buses, the driver reads space like a map

of what isn't but might be about to be, envisioning a lane just before it opens, Old Delhi,
my elbow two inches from a fender, he peddles sweating inside his sun-dark skin,

frayed shirt. He took us to the Red Fort, Moghul architecture, the Taj's cousin, palace
of the son who imprisoned his father who spent his days with courtesans and courtiers,

stories of ten thousand nights passed down on the wings of a roc, strong enough to lift
an elephant in its talons. In the Big Sur fire, rescued, a nest of six condors, two-month-olds

the size of chickens, can't yet fly, two died, pre-historic faces, black ruff of feathers,
ugly bald heads. In the big hill fire, one orange cat survived inside a brick chimney.

What does it mean when children eat ashes? All fall down, the plague ended when
the great Fire of London killed the rats. A cow kicked over a lantern to start the great

Chicago blaze. The Straw Man's fear of flames. Lightning set the hills crackling,
cinders, embers, umbrellas useless against atomic rain, gray Hiroshima cinder-flakes

falling for days. Little Japanese umbrella in the children's drinks, embroidered slippers,
tiny arches of the women's bound feet, smaller than half a hand, monkey's claw,

the expectations of beauty, retarded metatarsals in pain for life, disabled, carried, married
behind a red veil, unseen body, skin and its nakedness. As far back as the Gupta empire,

widows would immolate themselves on the husband's funeral pyre, at first, voluntarily,
later not. Bruno, memory expert, believing in an infinite, pantheistic, hylozoistic universe,

heliocentrism, metempsychosis and multiple worlds, was tried, placed in an iron gag,
a spike through his tongue, burned at the stake, combustible, our thoughts, words, flesh.

Evolution

We grew into creatures with thumbs, an appetite for meat, large brain-cases to
conjugate verbs: about to be, desiring to have been, wishing to have had the capacity

to become. Going from social primates to ground-dwelling, swelling with pride and warfare,
earning car-fare, telling bare-faced lies, kleptomaniacs of all we wish to have said, I stole

"myriad-minded" twice, trying to fathom the different forms of knowing, through body,
brain, book, skin, eyes designed for facial recognition at 50 feet. Are we safe here? Slippery

underbelly, sub-synaptical concepts swerve into layers of reference, that's why we wear shoes,
exposed soles do no good when walking somewhere, having gone, about to pack to go,

predictable, like a water table. I hated the sevens, especially nine times seven, oddities of mind
that make me me, and you have come to expect unfolding, unreeling spool, once known,

about to be forgotten and recycled in bits. My softest old orange sweatshirt in the rag-bin,
scraps for a quilt, for shoe polish, window wash, gazing glassy-eyed through the re-glazed

bay window to find the too-bright gold-flatware of the Bay lying there, streaming and about
to go cobalt. Archaea, single-celled without nuclei or organelles, thought to be extremophiles

(volcanic hot springs, salt lakes), now found in the mammalian gut, maybe earth's oldest
lineage. He said the problem with the financial markets is the lack of transparency,

everything too abstract, no product, no value. Human history, 200,000 years, a drop
in time's bucket, paleoanthropologists argue over the archaic species, whether Neanderthals

coexisted with the lost branches, pygmy genome sequencing, other groups speaking click
languages share some odd DNA sequences, ancestral history hidden in the mitochondria.

Orangutans predate the split, the point where the human line diverged, proto-primates
appeared in the Paleocene, first hominids in the Miocene, Plesiadapis, an archaic primate

60 million years ago in Wyoming. Grooming builds not only social structure, but tactile
relationships, skin to skin, how the mother meets the baby these days, back again to where

we were before the isolette. The monkeysphere is the number a primate can track in
her social group, and reflects the size of cortex, as it grows, so does verbal communication.

Now that we're we, picking our nits and talking, roots and leaf, the chewy bark, babies
clinging to the under-fur, swing and sit, launch and sleep, dreaming the circuits

of the excitable mind, going far, wire to wire, disinvited from the tree of being, fall
to ground. The gorilla mother carried her dead baby around for weeks, unwilling to give

it up, unable to comprehend? or waiting for resuscitation? We recite prayers waiting for
the coma to pass. It never does, we carry it inside, unknowing, glued synapse, the dead

and held collective ghost we resemble in our darker moments. Whish of skirt on floor
in the unlit hallway, night breeze blowing before sun up, before the air rinses into

lavender and cerulean, and our lidded eyes open to what is and isn't, one branch, in
the attic, a painted tree, grandmother's maiden name, Lemon, branching off

of Colton, Foster, twig and thumb. Further forms of being, is that up? or have we
merely forgotten the fullness of unconscious being, breathing in and the tree blows,

embryonic gill fronds, we all owned them in our prelapsarian archaic days, before
daylight, before The Beagle's voyage, the thin-inked notebooks of tortoises and

Galapagonian boobies, Darwin's concept of a tree just sprouting, now unteachable
in Kansas, vertebral column, fingerprints, the infant's random grin, one merged creature.

Metempsychosis, we recycle? Once I met him, psychosis became background music.
Begin in one shape then become another, experiencing a death in between or not.

Metamorphosis, separation is amnesia, Mrs. Orpheus sinking back into blackness,
while the singing goes on in her absence, peculiar intertwining of words and music,

particular melody, particulate phonemes, particle accelerator of the mind, amygdala,
almond-shape, point where the limbic's archaic emotions meet up with perception,

doors flung open, baby melds with adult, nucleus of association, slung out on the long
wires, glossy myelin sheaths, full of the nothing we came from, the everything we

aspired to before realizing it probably wasn't going to happen. Instead, down this
side-chain, daily being and dinner, lo mein and sea weed, flavored with black egg,

parental DNA saturating the templates of reaction and interaction, we came to a fork
in the road, arriving here, stucco and red tile, bay fog, monkey mien. I remember you.

Limit

Reeling downhill between snowbanks at 70 mph wide sweep of a turn following red
tail lights, how do the dotted white lines hold you? What holds? Yoga, letting your

mind sink into the tube of your breathing, pipeline, those giant wave surfers riding
the funnel of a 50' wave, towed there and let fly, perched on a moment of momentum

and balance, the speed of sinking and forward propulsion counter-weighed to the width
of a second, breath inside that space, going, gone. The mind likes to seep out between

twigs of hedges, between bamboo stalks and go roaming, looking for its own self
whom it loves richly and never quite finds, elusive as snow leopard, as white fox hidden

in obvious surroundings, the eye can't keep up with the mind, even knowing its pores,
paces, fancy footwork, hiding in plain sight, play side-A again, flipside, something darker,

no one remembers its name. I called you. No answer. The body left on the floor breathing,
hands full of yarrow sticks casting the future, fins of aquatic creatures holding their balance

in space, sinking and floating away. Did you mean me? When I'm cranky, you say "Don't blame
me, I voted for you." Poor iridescent fish, flapping away, land-locked. Limitations of movement

in three dimensions, out of reach of one whose feet tend not to leave the ground except
in sleep. Probably this overflow of longing propels into the waves of indulgence, greedy: more—

more time, more than what is commonly believed to be humanly possible. Out on the limb of
probability, reel it in, human as a leaf, veins and interstices, sun-food, photochemicals, we see

and we eat, we're all sunlight in one form or another, the present is the mind, what it does with light
bouncing off remembered surfaces. When chaos reaches its limit, peace begins to be restored.

Divination, gauging the harmony of the spheres, when blackness covers, light begins to manifest, the new moon fills in, absence is the fullest belly of the gray circle's shadow, empty

is the heat of our intention which becomes full in its phase. The I in I Ching means both easy and change, the book of changes. One state is eye and mouth, the face, the gaze,

swallowing, reaching form below working-form, embryo, the arms of an individual become chance, chase, the feel of feeling human. Mostly-black moon, Pleiades, night sky clotted

at altitude, blank filled with white, no empty space, explosions everywhere. Something firing inside the nothing, change is made of real sparks, quarks that morph, shape of matter,

the small obsessing, clinging, loving self, the reach towards, beyond. I felt your heart skip beats and considered if you would survive the night, if I would wake beside a quiet corpse

remembering the smells of last evening, zucchini and mushrooms, wine and chicken thighs, soy sauce and what's left from the day of fields of slushy snow in the crusted forest,

pine scent, amber light of evening, your going outside in the snow-filled meadow for chi-gung and my yellow pad indoors. Whiff of oolong and limits, edges of sun and surface, hide

and skin, falling hair, gray, lines, synapses that miss their beat. I forgot, I meant to love you, but I started humming instead. Leaves, the sky's gray water, old time, bristling

stars, skin so warm and smoky, scented like something from another world. I meant you. You meant me. We came here solitary under galaxies, the celestial is everyday, our fingers

interlocking, veins emerging on the backs of hands, mind loosening around the edges, marked seasons, wanting more. The ear swings on an inch of meaning, seeing into time.

ALICE JONES's collections of poetry from Alice James Books are *The Knot* which won the Beatrice Hawley Award, and *Isthmus*, winner of the Jane Kenyon Chapbook Award. *Extreme Directions (The fifty four moves of Tai Chi Sword)* was published by Omnidawn Press. Books from Apogee Press are *Gorgeous Mourning* and *Plunge*, a finalist for the Northern California Book Award in Poetry.

Awards include fellowships from the Bread Loaf Writers Conference and the National Endowment for the Arts, the First Annual Narrative Magazine Poetry Prize, and the Robert H. Winner and Lyric Poetry Awards from the Poetry Society of America.

After practicing internal medicine, she sought further training in psychiatry and psychoanalysis, which she now practices in Berkeley. She is a training and supervising analyst at the San Francisco Center for Psychoanalysis.

OTHER POETRY TITLES FROM APOGEE PRESS

TO ORDER OR FOR MORE
INFORMATION GO TO
WWW.APOGEEPRESS.COM

MAXINE CHERNOFF
Among the Names
The Turning

VALERIE COULTON
The Cellar Dreamer
open book
passing world pictures

TSERING WANGMO DHOMPA
In the Absent Everyday
My rice tastes like the lake
Rules of the House

KATHLEEN FRASER
Discrete Categories Forced into
Coupling

PAUL HOOVER
Edge and Fold

ALICE JONES
Gorgeous Mourning
Plunge

STEFANIE MARLIS
cloudlife
fine

A MAXWELL
Peeping Mot

EDWARD KLEINSCHMIDT MAYES
Speed of Life
To Whom it May Concern

PATTIE MCCARTHY
bk of (h)rs
marybones
Quiet Book
Table Alphabetical of Hard Words
Verso

DENISE NEWMAN
Future People
Human Forest
Wild Goods

ELIZABETH ROBINSON
Also Known As
Apostrophe
Apprehend

EDWARD SMALLFIELD
equinox
The Pleasures of C
to whom it may concern

COLE SWENSEN
Oh

BARBARA TOMASH
Arboreal

TRUONG TRAN
dust and conscience
four letter words
placing the accents
within the margin

LAURA WALKER
Follow-Haswed
story

KHATY XIONG
Poor Anima